THE MAN WHO PHOTOGRAPHED THE WORLD
BURTON HOLMES · TRAVELOGUES 1886-1938

Selected and edited by Genoa Caldwell   Introduction by Irving Wallace

THE MAN WHO PHOTOGRAPHED

Harry N. Abrams, Inc.,

THE WORLD BURTON HOLMES TRAVELOGUES 1886-1938

Publishers, New York

ACKNOWLEDGMENTS

I wish to thank the following people for their help in making this book a reality: Robert Mallett and Robert Hollingsworth, of The Burton Holmes Organization; Irving Wallace, for his encouragement and the use of his article; Greg Brull of the Burton Holmes Lab; Paul, Mark, and Louis, of Still Photo Lab, and Tom Ikemaya, of Chroma-Lab, for their fine prints; DeRutter Jones and Jeanne Shea, for their excellent editorial assistance; Margaret L. Kaplan and Robert Morton of Harry N. Abrams, Inc., for being as wildly enthusiastic about the project as I; Brooks Caldwell, my friend and husband, my inspiration.

And, finally, I would like to thank Burton Holmes, whose expertise with a camera, combined with his brilliance with a pen, made putting this book together a real joy.

Genoa Caldwell

Editor: Margaret L. Kaplan
Book design: Wei-Wen Chang
Library of Congress Cataloging in Publication Data

Holmes, Burton,
Burton Holmes: the man who photographed the world.

Includes index.
1. Holmes, Burton, 1870–   2. Travelers—United States—Biography. I. Caldwell, Genoa. II. Title.
G226.H6A32   779'.9'910924   77-8075
ISBN 0-8109-1059-4
Library of Congress Catalogue Card Number: 77-8075

Published in 1977 by Harry N. Abrams, Incorporated, New York
All rights reserved. No part of the contents of this book may be reproduced without the written permission of the publishers

Printed and bound in the United States of America

CONTENTS

EVERYBODY'S ROVER BOY

BY IRVING WALLACE

The following appreciation is excerpted from an article written by
Irving Wallace and incorporated in his book *The Sunday Gentleman*.
The article was written some eleven years before Burton Holmes's
death. Since I believe that it provides the best view of Burton
Holmes that exists, it stands as it was written in 1947.

GENOA CALDWELL

Burton Holmes in the bedroom of his boyhood home in Chicago, 1906.

One day in the year 1890, Miss Nellie Bly, of the New York *World*, came roaring into Brooklyn on a special train from San Francisco. In a successful effort to beat Phileas Fogg's fictional 80 days around the world, Miss Bly, traveling with two handbags and flannel underwear, had circled the globe in 72 days, 6 hours, and 11 minutes. Immortality awaited her.

Elsewhere that same year, another less-publicized globe-girdler made his start toward immortality. He was Mr. Burton Holmes, making his public debut with slides and anecdotes ("Through Europe With a Kodak") before the Chicago Camera Club. Mr. Holmes, while less spectacular than his feminine rival, was destined, for that very reason, soon to dethrone her as America's number-one traveler.

Today, Miss Bly and Mr. Holmes have one thing in common: In the mass mind they are legendary vagabonds relegated to the dim and dusty past of the Iron Horse and the paddle-wheel steamer. But if Miss Bly, who shuffled off this mortal coil in 1922, is now only a part of our folklore, there are millions to testify that Mr. Burton Holmes, aged seventy-six, is still very much with us.

Remembering that Mr. Holmes was an active contemporary of Miss Bly's, that he was making a livelihood at traveling when William McKinley, John L. Sullivan, and Admiral Dewey ruled the United States, when Tony Pastor, Lily Langtry, and Lillian Russell ruled the amusement world, it is at once amazing and reassuring to pick up the daily newspapers of 1946 and find, sandwiched between advertisements of rash young men lecturing on "Inside Stalin" and "I Was Hitler's Dentist," calm announcements that tomorrow evening Mr. Burton Holmes has something more to say about "Beautiful Bali."

Burton Holmes, a brisk, immaculate, chunky man with gray Vandyke beard, erect bearing, precise speech ("Folks are always mistaking me for Monty Woolley," he says, not unhappily), is one of the seven wonders of the entertainment world. As Everyman's tourist, Burton Holmes has crossed the Atlantic Ocean thirty times, the Pacific Ocean twenty times, and has gone completely around the world six times. He has spent fifty-five summers abroad, and recorded a half million feet of film of those summers. He was the first person to take motion picture cameras into Russia and Japan. He witnessed the regular decennial performance of the Passion Play at Oberammergau in 1890, and attended the first modern Olympics at Athens in 1896. He rode on the first Trans-Siberian train across Russia, and photographed the world's first airplane meet at Rheims.

As the fruit of these travels, Burton Holmes has delivered approximately 8,000 illustrated lectures that have grossed, according to an estimate by *Variety,* five million dollars in fifty-three winters. Because he does not like to be called a lecturer—"I'm a performer," he insists, "and I have performed on more legitimate stages than platforms"—he invented the word "travelogue" in London to describe his activity.

His travelogues, regarded as a fifth season of the year in most communities, have won him such popularity that he holds the record for playing in the longest one-man run in American show business. In the five and a half decades past, Burton Holmes has successively met the hectic competition of big-time vaudeville, stage, silent pictures, radio, and talking pictures, and he has survived them all.

At an age when most men have retired to slippered ease or are grounded by high blood pressure, Burton Holmes is more active and more popular than ever before. In the season just finished, which he started in San Francisco during September, 1945, and wound up in New York during April, 1946, Holmes appeared in 187 shows, a record number. He averaged six travelogues a week, spoke for two hours at each, and did 30 percent more box-office business than five years ago. Not once was a scheduled lecture postponed or canceled. In fact, he has missed only two in his life. In 1935, flying over the Dust Bowl, he suffered laryngitis and was forced to bypass two college dates. He has never canceled an appearance before a paid city audience. Seven years ago, when one of his elderly limbs was fractured in an automobile crack-up in Finland, there was a feeling that Burton Holmes might not make the rounds. When news of the accident was released, it was as if word had gone out that Santa Claus was about to cancel his winter schedule. But when the 1939 season dawned, Burton Holmes rolled on the stage in a wheelchair, and from his seat of pain (and for 129 consecutive appearances thereafter), he delivered his travel chat.

Before World War II, accompanied by Margaret Oliver, his wife of thirty-two years, Holmes would spend his breathing spells on summery excursions through the Far East or Europe.

Months later, he would communicate his findings to his cult, at a maximum price of $1.50 per seat. With the outbreak of war, Holmes changed his pattern. He curtailed travel outside the Americas. This year, except for one journey to Las Vegas, Nevada, where he personally photographed cowboy cutups and shapely starlets at the annual Helldorado festival, Holmes has been allowing his assistants to do all his traveling for him.

When he travels, he thinks he will visit three of the four accessible places on earth that he has not yet seen. One is Tahiti, which he barely missed a dozen times, and the other two are Iran and Iraq. The remaining country that he has not seen, and has no wish to see, is primitive Afghanistan. Of all cities on earth, he would most like to revisit Kyoto, once capital of Japan. He still recalls that the first movies ever made inside Japan were ones he made in Kyoto, in 1899. The other cities he desires to revisit are Venice and Rome. The only island for which he has any longing is Bali—"the one quaint spot on earth where you can really get away from it all."

Every season presents its own obstacles, and the next will challenge Holmes with a new audience of travel-sated and disillusioned ex-GI's. Many of these men, and their families, now know that a South Sea island paradise means mosquitoes and malaria and not Melville's Fayaway and Loti's Rarahu. They know Europe means mud and ruins and not romance. Nevertheless, Holmes is confident that he will win these people over.

"The veterans of World War II will come to my travelogues just as their fathers did. After the First World War, I gave illustrated lectures on the sights of

Grandma Burton on her birthday, 1908. The picture was made in her suite in the Congress Hotel, Chicago.

France, and the ex-doughboys enjoyed them immensely. But I suppose there's no use comparing that war to this. The First World War was a minor dispute between gentlemen. In this one, the atrocities and miseries will be difficult to forget. I know I can't give my Beautiful Italy lecture next season to men who know Italy only as a pigsty, but you see, in my heart Italy is forever beautiful, and I see things in Italy they can't see, poor fellows. How could they? ... Still, memory is frail, and one day these boys will forget and come to my lectures not to hoot but to relive the better moments and enjoy themselves."

Once Holmes takes to the road for his regular season, he is a perpetual-motion machine. Leaving his wife behind, he barnstorms with his manager, Everest, and a projectionist, whirling to Western dates in his Cadillac, making long hops by plane, following the heavier Eastern circuit by train. Holmes likes to amaze younger men with his activities during a typical week. If he speaks in Detroit on a Tuesday night, he will lecture in Chicago on Wednesday evening, in Milwaukee on Thursday, be back in Chicago for Friday evening and a Saturday matinee session, then go on to Kansas City on Sunday, St. Louis on Monday, and play a return engagement in Detroit on Tuesday.

This relentless merry-go-round (with Saturday nights off to attend a newsreel "and see what's happening in the world") invigorates Holmes, but grinds his colleagues to a frazzle. One morning last season, after weeks of trains and travel, Walter Everest was awakened by a porter at six. He rose groggily, sat swaying on the edge of his berth trying to pull on his shoes. He had the look of a man who had pushed through the Matto Grosso on foot. He glanced up sleepily, and there, across the aisle, was Holmes, fully dressed, looking natty and refreshed. Holmes smiled

sympathetically. "I know, Walter," he said, "this life *is* tiring. One day both of us ought to climb on some train and get away from it all."

Born in January, 1870, of a financially secure, completely cosmopolitan Chicago family, he was able to be independent from his earliest days. His father, an employee in the Third National Bank, distinguished himself largely by lending George Pullman enough cash to transform his old day coaches into the first Pullman Palace Sleeping Cars, and by refusing a half interest in the business in exchange for his help. Even to this day, it makes Burton Holmes dizzy to think of the money he might have saved in charges for Pullman berths.

Holmes's interest in show business began at the age of nine when his grandmother, Ann W. Burton, took him to hear John L. Stoddard lecture on the Passion Play at Oberammergau. Young Holmes was never the same again. After brief visits to faraway Florida and California, he quit school and accompanied his grandmother on his first trip abroad. He was sixteen and wide-eyed. His grandmother, who had traveled with her wine-salesman husband to France and Egypt and down the Volga in the sixties, was the perfect guide. But this journey through Europe was eclipsed, four years later, by a more important pilgrimage with his grandmother to Germany. The first day at his hotel in Munich, Holmes saw John L. Stoddard pass through the lobby reading a Baedeker. He was petrified. It was as if he had seen his Maker. Even now, over a half century later, when Holmes speaks about Stoddard, his voice carries a tinge of awe. For eighteen years of the late nineteenth century, Stoddard, with black-and-white slides and magnificent oratory, dominated the travel-lecture field. To audiences, young and old, he was the most romantic figure in America. Later, at Oberammergau, Holmes sat next to Stoddard through the fifteen acts of the Passion Play and they became friends.

When Holmes returned to the States, some months after Nellie Bly had made her own triumphal return to Brooklyn, he showed rare Kodak negatives of his travels to fellow members of the Chicago Camera Club. The members were impressed, and one suggested that these be mounted as slides and shown to the general public. "To take the edge off the silence, to keep the show moving," says Holmes, "I wrote an account of my journey and read it, as the stereopticon man changed slides." The show, which grossed the club $350, was Holmes's initial travelogue. However, he dates the beginning of his professional career from three years later, when he appeared under his own auspices with hand-colored slides.

After the Camera Club debut, Holmes did not go immediately into the travelogue field. He was not yet ready to appreciate its possibilities. Instead, he attempted to sell real estate, and failed. Then he worked for eight dollars a week as a photo supply clerk. In 1892, aching with wanderlust, he bullied his family into staking him to a five-month tour of Japan. On the boat he was thrilled to find John L. Stoddard, also bound for Japan. They became closer friends, even though they saw Nippon through different eyes. "The older man found Japan queer, quaint, comfortless, and almost repellent," Stoddard's son wrote years later. "To the younger man it was a fairyland." Stoddard invited Holmes to continue on around the world with him, but Holmes loved Japan and decided to remain.

When Holmes returned to Chicago, the World's Columbian Exposition of 1893 was in full swing. He spent months at the Jackson Park grounds, under Edison's new electric lights, listening to Lillian Russell

sing, Susan B. Anthony speak, and watching Sandow perform feats of strength. With rising excitement, he observed Jim Brady eating, Anthony Comstock snorting at Little Egypt's hootchy-kootchy, and Alexander Dowie announcing himself as the Prophet Elijah III.

In the midst of this excitement came the depression of that year. Holmes's father suffered. "He hit the wheat pit at the wrong time, and I had to go out on my own," says Holmes. "The photo supply house offered me fifteen dollars a week to return. But I didn't want to work. The trip to Japan, the Oriental exhibits of the Exposition, were still on my mind. I thought of Stoddard. I thought of the slides I'd had hand-colored in Tokyo. That was it, and it wasn't work. So I hired a hall and became a travel lecturer."

Copying society addresses from his mother's visiting list, and additional addresses from *The Blue Book,* Holmes mailed two thousand invitations in the form of Japanese poem-cards. Recipients were invited to two illustrated lectures, at $1.50 each, on "Japan—the Country and the Cities." Both performances were sell-outs. Holmes grossed $700.

For four years Holmes continued his fight to win a steady following, but with only erratic success. Then, in 1897, when he stood at the brink of defeat, two events occurred to change his life. First, John L. Stoddard retired from the travel-lecture field and threw the platforms of the nation open to a successor. Second, Holmes supplemented colored slides with a new method of illustrating his talks. As his circular announced, "There will be presented for the first time in connection with a course of travel lectures a series of pictures to which a modern miracle has added the illusion of life itself—the reproduction of recorded motion."

Armed with his jumpy movies—scenes of the Omaha fire department, a police parade in Chicago,

Mount Fuji.

Italians eating spaghetti, each reel running twenty-five seconds, with a four-minute wait between reels—Burton Holmes invaded the Stoddard strongholds in the East. Stoddard came to hear him and observe the newfangled movies. Like Marshal Foch, who regarded the airplane as "an impractical toy," Stoddard saw no future in the motion picture. Nevertheless, he gave young Holmes a hand by insisting that Augustin Daly lease his Manhattan theater to the newcomer. This done, Stoddard retired to the Austrian Tyrol, and Holmes went on to absorb Stoddard's audiences in Boston and Philadelphia and to win new followers of his own throughout the nation.

His success assured, Holmes began to gather material with a vigor that was to make him one of history's most indefatigable travelers. In 1900, at the Paris Exposition, sitting in a restaurant built like a Russian train, drinking vodka while a colored panorama of Siberia rolled past his window, he succumbed to this unique advertising of the new Trans-Siberian railway and bought a ticket. The trip in 1901 was a nightmare. After ten days on the Trans-Siberian train, which banged along at eleven miles an hour, Holmes was dumped into a construction train for five days, and then spent twenty-seven days on steamers going down the Amur River. It took him forty-two and a half days to travel from Moscow to Vladivostok.

But during that tour, he had one great moment. He saw Count Leo Tolstoi at Yasnaya Polyana, the author's country estate near Tula. At a dinner in Moscow, Holmes met Albert J. Beveridge, the handsome senator from Indiana. Beveridge had a letter of introduction to Tolstoi and invited Holmes and his enormous 60-mm movie camera to come along. Arriving in a four-horse landau, the Americans were surprised to find Tolstoi's estate dilapidated. Then, they were kept waiting two hours. At last, the seventy-three-year-old, white-bearded Tolstoi, nine years away from his lonely death in a railway depot, appeared. He was attired in a mujik costume. He invited his visitors to breakfast, then conversed in fluent English. "He had only a slight accent, and he spoke with the cadence of Sir Henry Irving," Holmes recalls.

Of the entire morning's conversation, Holmes remembers clearly only one remark. That was when Tolstoi harangued, "There should be no law. No man should have the right to judge or condemn another. Absolute freedom of the individual is the only thing that can redeem the world. Christ was a great teacher, nothing more!" As Tolstoi continued to speak, Holmes quietly set up his movie camera. Tolstoi had never seen one before. He posed stiffly, as for a daguerreotype. When he thought that it was over, and resumed his talking, Holmes began actual shooting. This priceless film never reached the screen. Senator Beveridge was then a presidential possibility. His managers feared that this film of Beveridge with a Russian radical might be used by his opponents. The film was taken from Holmes and destroyed.* Later, when he was not even nominated for the presidency, Beveridge wrote an apology to Holmes, "for this destruction of so valuable a living record of the grand old Russian."

In 1934, at a cost of ten dollars a day, Holmes spent twenty-one days in modern Soviet Russia. He loved the ballet, the omelets, the Russian rule against tipping, and the lack of holdups. He went twice to see the embalmed Lenin, fascinated by the sight of "his head resting on a red pillow like that of a tired man asleep."

*Editor's Note: Holmes took both stills and motion picture film during the Tolstoi meeting. Beveridge believed that the motion picture film was destroyed, and because members of his family were still alive at this writing Holmes let the myth stand. Holmes retained a print and stills of that film that exist today.

Spectators at a police parade in Chicago, 1893.

Burton Holmes breakfasts at a table transferred from the Café de la Paix to Topside, his home in Hollywood, 1951.

Although Holmes's name had already appeared on eighteen travel volumes, this last Russian trip inspired him to write his first and only original book. The earlier eighteen volumes were offered as a set, of which over forty thousand were sold. However, they were not "written," but were actually a collection of lectures delivered orally by Holmes. The one book that he wrote as a book, *The Traveler's Russia,* published in 1934 by G. P. Putnam's Sons, was a failure. Holmes has bought the remainders and passes them out to guests with a variety of inscriptions. In a serious mood he will inscribe, "To travel is to possess the world." In a frivolous mood, he will write, "With love from Tovarich Burtonovich Holmeski."

In the five decades past, Holmes has kept himself occupied with a wide variety of pleasures, such as attending Queen Victoria's Golden Jubilee in London, chatting with Admiral Dewey in Hong Kong, driving the first automobile seen in Denmark, and photographing a mighty eruption of Vesuvius.

In 1918, wearing a war correspondent's uniform, he shot army scenes on the Western Front and his films surpassed those of the poorly organized newsreel cameramen. In 1923, flying for the first time, he had his most dangerous experience, when his plane almost crashed between Toulouse and Rabat. Later, in Berlin, he found his dollar worth ten million marks, and in Africa he interviewed Emperor Haile Selassie in French, and, closer to home, he flew 20,000 miles over Central and South America.

Burton Holmes enjoys company on his trips. By coincidence, they are often celebrities. Holmes traveled through Austria with Maria Jeritza, through Greece with E.F. Benson, through the Philippines with Dr. Victor Heiser. He covered World War I with Harry Franck, wandered about Japan with Lafcadio Hearn's son, crossed Ethiopia with the Duke of Gloucester. He saw Hollywood with Mary Pickford, Red Square with Alma Gluck, and the Andes with John McCutcheon.

Of the hundreds of travelogues that Holmes has delivered, the most popular was "The Panama Canal." He offered this in 1912, when the "big ditch" was under construction, and news-hungry citizens flocked to hear him. Among less timely subjects, his most popular was the standard masterpiece on Oberammergau, followed closely by his illustrated lectures on the "Frivolities of Paris," the "Canals of Venice," the "Countryside of England" and, more currently, "Adventures in Mexico." Burton Holmes admits that his greatest failure was an elaborate travelogue on Siam, even though it seemed to have everything except Anna and the King thereof. Other failures included travelogues on India, Burma, Ethiopia, and—curiously—exotic Bali. The only two domestic subjects to fizzle were "Down in Dixie" in 1915 and "The Century of Progress Exposition" in 1933.

For a while, Hollywood appeared to be the travelogue's greatest threat. Holmes defeated this menace by marriage with the studios. He signed a contract with Paramount, made fifty-two travel shorts each year, between 1915 and 1921. Then, with the advent of talking pictures, Holmes joined Metro-Goldwyn-Mayer and made a series of travelogues, released in English, French, Italian, Spanish. In 1933, he made his debut in radio, and in 1944 made his first appearance on television.

Today, safe in the knowledge that he is an institution, Holmes spends more and more time in his rambling, plantation-style, wooden home, called "Topside," located on a hill a mile above crowded Hollywood Boulevard. This dozen-roomed brown house, once a riding club for silent-day film stars, and owned for six years by Francis X. Bushman (who gave it Hollywood's first swimming pool, where Holmes now permits neighborhood children to splash), was purchased by Holmes in 1930. "I had that M-G-M contract," he says, "and it earned me a couple of hundred thousand dollars. Well, everyone with a studio contract immediately gets himself a big car, a big house, and a small blonde. I acquired the car, the house, but kept the blonde a mental acquisition." For years, Holmes also owned a Manhattan duplex decorated with costly Japanese and Buddhist treasures, which he called "Nirvana." Before Pearl Harbor, Holmes sold this duplex, with its two-million-dollar collection of furnishings, to Robert Ripley, the cartoonist and oddity hunter.

Now, in his rare moments of leisure, Holmes likes to sit on the veranda of his Hollywood home and chat with his wife. Before he met her, he had been involved in one public romance. Gossips, everywhere, insisted that he might marry the fabulous Elsie de Wolfe, actress, millionaire decorator, friend of Oscar Wilde and Sarah Bernhardt, who later became Lady Mendl. Once, in Denver, Holmes recalls, a reporter asked him if he was engaged to Elsie de Wolfe. Holmes replied, curtly, No. That afternoon a banner headline proclaimed: BURTON HOLMES REFUSES TO MARRY ELSIE DE WOLFE!

Shortly afterward, during a photographic excursion, Holmes met Margaret Oliver, who, suffering from deafness, had taken up still photography as an avocation. In 1914, following a moonlight proposal on a steamer's deck, he married Miss Oliver in New York City's St. Stephen's Episcopal Church, and took her to prosaic Atlantic City for the first few days of their honeymoon, then immediately embarked on a long trip abroad.

When his wife is out shopping, Holmes will stroll about his estate, study his fifty-four towering palm trees, return to the veranda for a highball, thumb through the *National Geographic,* play with his cats, or pick up a language textbook. He is on speaking terms with eight languages including some of the Scandinavian, and is eager to learn more. He never reads travel books. "As Pierre Loti once remarked, 'I don't read. It might ruin my style,' " he explains.

He likes visitors, and he will startle them with allusions to his earlier contemporaries. "This lawn party reminds me of the one at which I met Emperor Meiji," he will say. Meiji, grandfather of Hirohito, opened Japan to Commodore Perry. When visitors ask for his travel advice, Holmes invariably tells them to see the Americas first. "Why go to Mont St. Michel?" he asks. "Have you seen Monticello?"

But when alone with his wife and co-workers on the veranda, and the pressure of the new season is weeks away, he will loosen his blue dressing gown, inhale, then stare reflectively out over the sun-bathed city below.

"You know, this is the best," he will say softly, "looking down on this Los Angeles. It is heaven. I could sit here the rest of my life." Then, suddenly, he will add, "There is so much else to see and do. If only I could have another threescore years upon this planet. If only I could know the good earth better than I do."

He lived long, but he died soon enough—certainly soon enough to avoid the ignominious end of fading into obscurity. Burton Holmes did not outlive his audience, and so he escaped the cruel fate of becoming an anachronism. Instead, like Nellie Bly, he became an American legend, and as a legend, if not as a corporation, he will enjoy immortality.

"Everybody's Rover Boy" (originally "The Great Globe Trotter") was copyrighted in 1947 by the Curtis Publishing Company; it appeared in *The Sunday Gentleman,* and is here reprinted by permission of Irving Wallace. Bantam Books edition republished *The Sunday Gentleman* in 1976.

THE TRAVELOGUE MAN

BY GENOA CALDWELL

Travelogue—the gist of a journey, ground fine by discrimination, leavened with information, seasoned with humor, fashioned in literary form and embellished by pictures that delight the eye, while the spoken story charms the ear.

BURTON HOLMES

Burton Holmes's first photograph.

Burton Holmes purchased his first camera in 1883, and began a love affair with photography that lasted throughout his eighty-eight years. Almost equaling his passion for capturing life on film was a desire to travel—it didn't matter where, as long as when he got there life was interesting.

Holmes had an insatiable curiosity. He wanted to know what was on the other side of the ocean, beyond the next hill, behind the next tree. It didn't take him long, however, to find out that travel is expensive. He found the solution to his financial problems when he realized that others loved to travel to exotic places but didn't have the money, time, or stamina. There was a built-in audience for a person who would do the traveling for them and bring back words and pictures for their vicarious pleasure.

Holmes coined the word Travelogue. In those early days a Travelogue was not quite as it is thought of today. It was the grand event of the season, and Holmes played to audiences in evening dress who had paid upwards of a dollar and a quarter per person. And this was during the same period when the latest Hollywood movie could be seen for a dime.

That is the way most people remember Holmes: "The Travelogue Man." Yet it was Holmes the photographer who was far more interesting. He was totally dedicated to his craft, both artistically and technically. His early glass slides, which measured 3½ by 4½ inches, were exquisitely hand-painted in Japan by a team of woman artists. In later years, the painting was done in the United States by artists he himself trained. Much of the work was so fine that single-hair ermine brushes were used. So beautiful is the painting that many of the slides look as if they had been taken with the best modern color film. His black-and-white photographs have extraordinary sharpness and clarity even today. These technical achievements, combined with Holmes's unique eye for content, make him one of the world's outstanding photographers. He experimented constantly with photographic techniques, and was in close touch with the various companies that built his equipment, searching for ways to improve his pictures. He refined his camera through the years, and although it is bulky by today's standards, it is still quite modern.

That same dedication to technical innovation also explains why few people today have seen his work. He felt that while anyone could look at a small photograph and get a certain amount of value from it, how much more could be obtained if that same photograph were projected on a large screen. How much greater the effect on the senses; how much richer the colors. Coupled with the fact that a number of slides could be put through a projector at a given speed, along with narration, the whole photo essay could be absorbed without the need to look away from the photographs to read a text or turn a page. His method of display fulfilled both his needs and those of his audience, but it was of the moment and left nothing for History.

The Travelogue, then, held two functions for Holmes. It acted as a unique and totally engrossing one-man photo exhibit, and it generated funds for his next journey. Although he published many travel books, relatively few photographs appear in them, and only a small number have ever been reproduced outside of his own works. It is worthy of note that Holmes was also a pioneer in the field of documentary film, and in this area Burton Holmes International, an organization Holmes founded, has continued to function since his death. Their involvement in motion pictures and Holography has been so complete that it has remained until now for this book to be assembled.

Holmes's writings show a delightful sense of humor about himself, and ironically, when juxtaposed with the importance of his photography, a seemingly incongruous Holmes appears. Yet it is this seeming incongruity that is the essence of his personality: a man of tremendous knowledge who yet retained a true innocence.

Ahead of you lies a chronological journey around the world from 1886, when Holmes first began traveling with a camera, through 1938. Because of World War II and Holmes's advanced age, his true creativity slowed down significantly at this time, and although he worked on, writing and lecturing until shortly before his death in 1958, his best photographic years were behind him.

GENOA CALDWELL

EARLY YEARS 1883–1900

BY BURTON HOLMES

There was for me the fascination of magic in photography. There were then few amateur photographers. The layman knew nothing of darkroom mysteries. The word Kodak had not yet been coined. You could not press the button and let someone else do the rest. You had to do it all yourself and know what you were doing.

In 1883 I saw the earliest display of photographic apparatus "for the amateur" at the Old Illinois Industrial Exposition. I invested my savings in a $10.00 outfit. The camera was heavy and clumsy with six double holders for glass plates, 4 x 5 inches in size. The lens was a single lens with a fixed diaphragm. Exposure of several seconds was required in bright sunlight. I acquired the necessary developing trays, red lantern, chemicals and glass graduates for measuring and mixing the solutions. I made my first test exposures from a window, up one flight, and on my plate an image of the northwest corner of State and Jackson Streets appeared. Then, with freshly loaded holders, I set out for the Lake Front Park to make my first solo flight in photography. I sought a subject for my first photograph. My eyes lighted on a sleeping "bum" sprawled on an old park bench. I still possess the picture and it's not a bad one either. I did all the photographic work myself, developing, printing, mounting the prints, and became fairly expert at it.

My negatives had been made on what you might call paper film. There was no flexible celluloid then available. But the Eastman Company had turned out rolls of sensitized paper on which pictures could be taken, developed and then cut into single paper negatives. But, of course, prints or slides could not be made from them, the grain of the paper would have been too conspicuous. A transfer of the image to a transparent medium was necessary; so the paper negatives were placed face down on the glass plates coated with collodion. Then the paper was removed and the emulsion with the negative image on it was transferred by a sort of decalcomania process to a stiff sheet of fairly transparent celluloid, and behold, the first film negatives. All the developing and transferring I did myself in the darkroom of the Chicago Camera Club. There I made glass slides from my transferred paper negatives.

When I was ten, I thought I'd like to be a magician. I had from infancy been fond of doing tricks. I have been told, I don't remember much about it, that at the age of five I had my box of simple tricks and gave shows for family and friends. We lived then at the Old Clifton House on Wabash Avenue. Among the guests of that hotel, of which my father was co-proprietor, was a young attorney with a wife but no children. The couple took a fancy to me, so I'm told, and frequently, carrying my table of tricks, I would knock at their door and say, "I've come to give a show for you." After the performance, the young lawyer would take me on his knee and tell me what a wonderful bamboozler I was for my age. This compliment always pleased me. It still pleases me. The young lawyer's name was William McKinley.

Pursuing later my ambition to become a bigger and better bamboozler, I diligently studied the works of Robert Houdin, and haunted all the performances of Hermann the Great with my good friends George Hale, the future great astronomer, and Alfred McEwen. We knew all his tricks but marveled at his uncanny skill. He was the Paderewski of his art. Proudly we would march up to the stage when he called for volunteers to "assist" him. He came to recognize us as amateurs in his art and in later seasons even trusted us

to act as "plants" in the audience and take a really active part in his illusions. Many were the rabbits he pulled out of my coat. Alas, one night my rabbit, growing impatient, misbehaved; but I was proud to suffer damp inconvenience and tried to betray no visible concern.

At home, in an abandoned basement dining room, I rigged up a very pretentious little theater with a proscenium, a canton flannel curtain that rolled up and down, and the customary flashily decorated tables with traps in the tops and little unseen shelves on the sides away from the spectators. I called it "Le Theatre Magique" and there I put on shows that became better and better from year to year, selling tickets to family and friends.

After a strenuous rehearsal I was wont to sit alone, lights dimmed, surveying my trick tables and gaudy stage properties and dream of the time when I should be a real professional magician, touring the country like Hermann the Great, attracting large audiences and making oodles of money. I looked forward to the day when 8 P.M. would be the only hour with any meaning, when it would be the zero hour for me to go over the top with my first act to the music of the "Skaters Waltz," which Hermann always used as the theme music for his introductory sequence of illusions.

GOING ABROAD

When I decided to leave the Harvard School at the age of sixteen, the principal remonstrated with me. He said among other things, that if I did not carry on and go to college, there would be only one time when I

would regret it. Puzzled, I asked him when the one time would be. He answered, "All the time." Nevertheless I took my books home and a few weeks later my grand old grandmother, to my delight, asked me if I would care to go abroad with her for a few months. My mother went with us. We sailed on the flagship of the Cunard Line, the "Etruria," then the biggest, finest, fastest thing afloat and pride of the British mercantile marine. She was commanded by Captain Cook, the grim Commodore of the Cunard Line who was said to have boasted that he had never spoken to a mere passenger. At any rate he did not speak to us.

The first foreign soil on which I set foot was the "auld sod" of Erin. Setting foot was about all I did in Ireland; going ashore on the tender, standing on Irish soil for a few moments gave me my first thrill of being "otherwhere." The following day we landed, bag and baggage, in Liverpool.

I still recall with pleasure our first real meal ashore, the delicious English sole served at the Adelphi Hotel. I was not as favorably impressed by the plumbing of the hotel, and the heating and lighting devices left much to be desired. In a letter home, I declared that Europe was ages behind the U.S.A. in most things, but that I liked it nevertheless.

From Liverpool we traveled north to Edinburgh—my first foreign train. The Scottish Express seemed "dinky" to me after our, even then, vastly superior Pullman trains.

Edinburgh thrilled me. I nearly quarrelled with Grandma because she had allotted only two days to what was, to me, the most wonderful city I had ever seen. But she had her plans, her schedule, hard and fast as any ever devised in later days by Thomas Cook. And so away, skipping London and going direct to Brussels. Then to the Homburg Spa in Germany, where we made a long stay of perhaps a fortnight.

Homburg was then one of the fashionable centers of the Continent. It was *the* thing for Americans who had dashed in and out of the famous, interesting cities to go and "take the cure" or loaf around in the Casino gar-

dens and listen to the band. I forgave Grandma our long sojourn in uninteresting but delightful Homburg the day she finally decided to move on and said, "Now, Burtie, buy three tickets, second class, for Paris." Paris! I would gladly have traveled third class or on a bike or on foot. Paris at last! I knew my Paris in advance. Had I not read and re-read my Baedeker, the Bible of the traveler? Had I not studied the maps and plans? Did I not know that I could find my way to Notre Dame or to the Invalides (the Eiffel Tower had not yet been built) without asking anyone which way to go?

Our hotel was the old Hôtel de l'Athenée near the stage door of the Opéra. "Let me go out alone for my first day in Paris," I pleaded. "I want to find my way around and then I will be a good boy and be your beau for all the rest of the sight-seeing—but first I want to *find* places for myself."

What a memorable day it was. First to the Café de la Paix, to sit at a table on the sidewalk—at the corner table which, according to Parisians, stands on the spot where the axis of the Universe impinges upon Paris. For the true *boulevardier* that table marks the central spot of civilization. What I ordered as *consommation*, I cannot say. Probably my favorite predilection, a chocolate ice cream. Then from a bus-top I surveyed the boulevards, miles of boulevards—recognizing all the famous sights. Then for a panoramic survey of the city, I climbed one of the towers of Notre Dame, and then the Tour St. Jacques, the Bastille Column, and the Arc de Triomphe, all in one long day. Evening found me atop Montmartre, where as yet there stood no great domed church of the Sacre Coeur but near the base of the famous hill—the red wings of the Moulin Rouge revolved in all their alluring gyratory activity. My French—school French—was pretty bad but it sufficed. The Springtime of life in Paris!

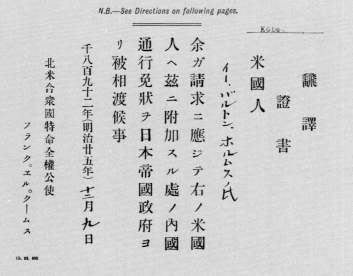

No. 1551

CERTIFICATE.

United States Legation,

TOKYO.

December 9th, 1892.

To whom it may Concern:

At my request the annexed Passport has been granted by the Imperial Japanese Government to the citizen of the United States undermentioned.

Frank L. Coombs,

Envoy Extraordinary and Minister Plenipotentiary of the United States.

Name of Bearer: Mr. E. Burton Holmes

N.B.—See Directions on following pages.

Kobe.

10. 92. 500

北米合衆國特命全權公使

フランク。エル。クームス

千八百九十二年（明治廿五年）十二月九日

余ガ請求ニ應ジテ右ノ米國人ヘ茲ニ附加スル處ノ內國通行免狀ヲ日本帝國政府ヨリ被相渡候事

イ、バルトン、ホルムス氏

米國人

證書

譯

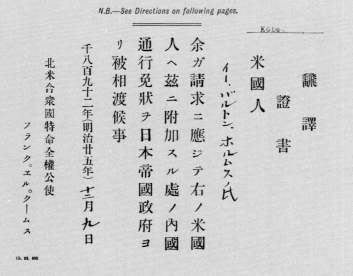

TRANSLATION OF THE REGULATIONS PRINTED IN JAPANESE ON BACK OF PASSPORT AND TO BE BORNE IN MIND BY THE BEARER.

I.—Foreigners traveling in the interior must obey all the local laws.

II.—They must set out within thirty days from the date of their Passports.

III.—Those foreigners who, on account of some difficulty encountered on the way, cannot return within the time fixed in their Passports shall, in due time, make known the cause of their detention, through their Ministers, to the Foreign Office.

IV.—Passports must be sent back within five days after the return of the holders. Those foreigners who set out from and return to such distant places as Nagasaki or Hakodate, must forward their Passports to the Foreign Office, through their Ministers, within thirty days.

V.—At hotels where they seek lodging, travelers will show their Passports to the hotel-keepers. Passports must also be shown by the way when requested for examination by the police, the Kuchō or the Kochō (heads of wards or districts). Foreigners who, on any account whatever, refuse to show their Passports shall be liable to arrest.

VI.—Passports are not transferable.

VII.—Foreigners who receive Passports to travel in the interior are not allowed to buy from, sell to, exchange, or make contracts with Japanese in any province.

VIII.—Foreigners who travel on Passports are not allowed to permanently dwell in houses of the Japanese in the interior.

IX.—Even those foreigners who have licenses to hunt are not allowed to shoot or hunt when they go beyond treaty limits.

X.—Foreigners who, on account of anything encountered in the journey, return after having gone part way and then wish to travel to the places left unvisited, shall return their Passports and obtain permission anew, even to visit places included in the Passport first procured by them.

XI.—Foreigners who violate any article written in their Passports, or in these regulations, shall for every offence be complained of by the Foreign Office to the Ministers of their countries.

NOTE.—The local laws above referred to forbid the following and similar acts:

1.—Traveling at night in a carriage without a light.
2.—Attending a fire on horseback.
3.—Disregarding notices of "No Thoroughfare."
4.—Rapid driving on narrow roads.
5.—Neglecting to pay ferry and bridge-tolls.
6.—Injuring notice boards, house signs and mile-posts.
7.—Scribbling on temples, shrines or walls.
8.—Injuring crops, shrubs, trees or plants on the roads or in gardens.
9.—Trespassing on fields, enclosures or game preserves.
10.—Lighting fires in woods or on hills or moors.

NOTICE TO AMERICAN CITIZENS APPLYING FOR TRAVELING PASSPORTS.

Applications for passports from American citizens must be made through the consulates, except when from residents in Tōkyō or the interior, and if for the first time must be accompanied with evidence of citizenship.

Each application should give the following information:

The name and present address of the applicant.

The route of travel and the principal places in the order in which they are to be visited. When covered by a fixed route, the number of the route only need be given.

The time, except in special cases, not exceeding three months.

The object, whether for health or scientific purposes.

Each application from a resident in Tōkyō or the interior should be accompanied by ten sen in stamps for the return postage, and the words "Application for Passport" should be written upon the cover.

These passports are good for one journey only, and the bearer must return to an open port before expiration unless otherwise authorized to reside in the interior.

Passports must be returned to the Legation within five days after expiration. In case of loss, notice of the same should at once be given, as a new passport will not be issued while there is one still outstanding.

While it is desirable that American citizens in Japanese employ should obtain their passports for travel from the Japanese authorities through the persons by whom they are employed, in special cases, however, passports may be obtained through the Legation. Such passports are only issued for a period of two weeks, except during the summer season, when the time is extended to two months.

I fell in love with the alluring Old Japan when I was twenty-two and very susceptible to the charm of things that were different. The Old Japan that I first knew was inconceivably picturesque, strangely and curiously beautiful. There were no ugly areas, no unfinished raw edges anywhere visible. All things Japanese were bound together into a satisfying mellow unity.

The world was then a free and friendly world, practically passportless until the advent of the World War of 1914 and the dawn of the Bureaucratic Era. But Japan, while admitting the stranger to certain specified ports, compelled him to secure a special passport for a journey into the interior. In due time my Japanese passport was delivered to me. It was a beautiful and curious document—and a very amusing one. It opened the gates of an oriental wonderland to me but it laid down rules for my behavior. I recall two positive prohibitions:

No foreigner shall attend a fire on horseback.

No foreigner shall go out at night without a lantern. There were other restrictions, but the first was the funniest of all. It did not make sense. It was very Japanese. I tried to explain it to myself. I decided that at some time in the past some excited "Ijin San," some "Honorable Foreign Devil," had ridden to a fire on horseback, injuring innocent bystanders in his haste to reach the scene of a catastrophe. The authorities had concluded that dashing to fires on horseback was a favorite American sport and therefore had made a solemn regulation curbing such performances in the name of public safety.

I have tried in vain to learn the Japanese language. But I did acquire a smattering of that exasperating tongue.

My accent and intonation were good—too good. They got me into trouble. So well did I pronounce the few words and phrases which I had learned that it was taken for granted that I spoke the language fluently. I once traveled through Japan with a man who was so accurate in his utterance of the words "So deska?" that the Japanese took him for a perfectionist in Nipponese and talked back to him in torrents.

"So deska?" means; "Is that so?" When anyone addressed us I would say modestly, "Wakarimasen"—"I don't understand." He would say with assurance, "SO, so deska?" and draw in his breath in the approved manner of a Japanese gentleman—and the conversation was on. When it seemed about to flag for want of more words from him, he would simply toss in another "So deska?"—inhale again—and the conversation took on new life. The trouble with me was that I would try to get back at them with a few remarks. That was where I gave myself away. I would try to be polite and use the more elegant form "Sayo de gozarimaska," which means the same thing. But old friend "So deska?" always won. To speak Japanese, you must be able to *think* the Japanese way. That is impossible.... You will find little help in dictionaries or phrase books. My first dip into a phrase book brought up a sentence in English for use at sea on a stormy day. "It is getting rough and I think I will go to bed." The Japanese form, literally translated was, "Ship tipsy have got, think little will lie." That is just a simple one. Here is a grander example which came into my young life at a Geisha party. One of the girls was strangely lovely with a beauty rarely seen in the Orient. I thought she was a peach. I wanted this conveyed to her. My guide-interpreter declined to pass it along, saying, "Please

no, she would not like it." He added in explanation, "We in Japan are not familiar with the form of fruit called peach and we do not like fruit anyway." But I wanted her to know that I regarded her as very beautiful and I insisted that my attendant Cyrano de Bergerac should voice my admiration in appropriate words. He did so. She nearly swooned with pleasure. "What were those words you used?" I eagerly inquired. "I may need them for some other occasion." I committed them to memory and used them frequently thereafter and always with pleasing results.

"Anata wa tamago ni me hana de gozarimas"—these are the magic words that will cause any musumé in Japan to think you know your stuff. What do they mean? You'd never guess. They mean, "You are an Egg with Eyes and Nose." How come that this, to us, insulting statement should delight a pretty girl? Should you call one of our girls an egg with eyes and nose, you might get a black eye and a broken nose. It is difficult to explain why "You are an Egg with Eyes and Nose" may be interpreted as "You are very beautiful, you have perfect features"—but to the Japanese, the implication of the phrase is crystal clear. Their ideal aristocratic face is an oval face with prominent features. The common face is round, flat, almost featureless. So take an egg, the perfect oval, give it bright sparkling eyes and a nose that *is* a nose and you have a face that will launch a thousand junks—or battleships.

Of aristocratic society in Japan I know nothing. But I

_____

◄ An old-time junk cuts an awkwardly graceful patch out of the very heart of the western sky. To me, there is more beauty in one of these slow, cumbersome out-of-date ships, with its crimped sails, than in the trimmest sloop that ever came from the genius of the best of modern designers.

have attended two Imperial garden parties. I have bowed low before two Emperors of Japan. I had to. Everybody else in sight was doing it and it would have been not only impolite but positively perilous not to conform to custom at the time. My genuflections were in both cases rather costly. I had to buy special clothes in order to be permitted to genuflect. The occasions on which I bent low before the Sons of Heaven were widely spaced. There was a span of thirty years between them. The first was in 1892, the second in 1922. The scene was, however, the same—the park of an Imperial Palace on the outskirts of Tokyo, where the annual Imperial garden parties were held.

It was not easy to get an invitation. You had to prove that you were really somebody. Then your Embassy or Legation would set in motion the machinery, which in due time would grind out a very elaborate card of invitation to view the Imperial chrysanthemums or to meet the Prince of Wales, as the case might be. But you had to be properly dressed and hatted for the occasion. That is where the high cost of being somebody came in. You simply had to wear a black frock coat, the kind known to our fathers as a Prince Albert. You had to wear a high silk hat. So far as this equipment was concerned, I had landed in Japan in the fall of 1892 practically nude. But as I scanned the coveted Imperial invitation—and read the rules of dress and behavior on the accompanying card, I decided that the show would be worth all that it promised to cost me. It was—definitely.

There were Chinese tailors in Yokohama who could make you a white duck suit overnight and for less than two dollars, gold. But a Prince Albert of broadcloth was another matter. I inquired if one could be created in time for the party. "Can do," was the reply.

Prince Albert, later Edward VII, would have been proud of that Chinese replica of his favorite formal garment. But securing the top hat was more difficult.

37

It called for a combing of all the hat shops in Yokohama. They had top hats in stock, but who would wear such antiquated modes? At last I dug up in a department store a topper that would have been O.K. on Fifth Avenue on Easter Sunday.

The question of spats had been left optional; but I was assured that a pair of spats, especially if white and conspicuous, would be a sort of passport to an advantageous position in the assembled mob of diplomats and honored guests at the imperial function. So spats it was—snowy white.

The party was an unforgettable event. So too was my progress from the Imperial Hotel to the Imperial Palace, which were several miles apart. It was an hour's run by riksha. Top hats, frock coats and rikshas do not mix but they do make a funny picture. I was not the only foreign "funny" on the way through town that day. Scores of equally ludicrous-looking "foreign devils" formed a miles-long comic strip, moving as fast as the stout legs of the kurumaya could propel them.

In the Palace park the scene was unbelievably comical. In 1892, the Japanese had not learned to wear "western clothes" properly. Such misfits, such collars, such neckties! Frock coats—and knickers!—silk hats so big they settled to the ears of the wearers! But the protocol demanded that all guests appear in costumes modeled after—a long way after—those which had been in vogue decades ago at the court of Queen Victoria. Thus garbed, we awaited the advent of the Imperial Family, Emperor and Empress, Ladies in Waiting, and court officials. The Mikado appeared in military uniform. The ladies looked like pictures torn from old copies of Godey's Ladies' Book.

Bustles are funny. As worn in Japan in 1892, they were a scream. The dainty Japanese ladies, who would have looked so charming in kimono, had adopted western fashions but not western manners. When they bowed, they bent forward at the waist, again and again,

jack-knife fashion. As their heads went down, up came the bustles. Oh, that the movies had been invented then!

Hirohito was acting as Regent in 1922, when I attended my second Imperial garden party held in honor of the Prince of Wales. The affair was not as funny as the first. The assembly was better dressed. I had a better frock coat and a better topper. The regent and his royal guest walked through the gardens, both looking very, very bored. The Empress Dowager and the court ladies were in out-moded European dress, but without bustles. We all bowed low as we had thirty years before. We all dashed for refreshments and finally, when the show was over, went back "down town"—to find the old Imperial Hotel in flames. I saw the final flaming crash of the grand old wooden structure. Police and firemen tried to stop me but I, in full garden party regalia, was not to be halted. They asked for credentials. I produced a metal disk, which they saluted. It was not a police badge. It was a big check for what I had left that morning in the hotel check-room. I never retrieved anything. But the check enabled me to witness from the very wet vantage point of a tangle of squirting fire hose, the utter destruction of the famous old hostelry—and all my other clothes and all the possessions of the members of the Prince's naval and military suite. We had lost all except the togs we had worn at the Garden Party. There was I on the scene of the catastrophe, all dressed up like a plush horse—with no place to go. There was then no other available

———————

Ethereal indeed this lovely mountain! Even on near ▶ approach it seems intangible, as if it were but an illusion built of violet mist and flecked with slender drifts of cloud.

hotel and the native inns were filled to overflowing. It was a case of "No Vacancy" in the Japanese Capital—except in the Yoshiwara. If you don't know what that means, look up the word; in a Japanese dictionary it means the "Place of Reeds." It means much more than that. Well, I had to lodge somewhere. I spent the night in one of the elaborate "night clubs" of the Nightless City.

I have come to Hokkaido to see the homes of a strange race, supposed to be the remnant of the aboriginal population of ancient Japan, a rapidly disappearing race called by the curious name of Ainu. There are only a few Ainu settlements left, even in Hokkaido, this island to which the survivors of a once numerous race have been driven by the smaller but more energetic Japanese, who overran the ancient Ainu archipelago. One of these settlements I found near a Japanese village known as Shiraoi. I expected to find the people living and dressing more or less like ordinary Japanese, but I was happily disappointed. The Ainu community of Shiraoi retains, perhaps more fully than any other, the curious characteristics of this very interesting race. I had always heard these people spoken of as the "Hairy Ainu." I must admit that they deserved the epithet, not because they are naturally hairy but because they make the most of all the hair that nature gives them—they do not cut it, they simply let it grow. The old men all have splendid patriarchal beards. Were it not for their peculiar costumes we might mistake their village council for a group of worthy Scottish elders. The scientific world is not agreed as to the race of these Ainu. Some say they are Mongolians, others say they are of our own Caucasian race.

Be that as it may, the Ainu is today a degenerate and disappearing race. Drink is responsible for this. They are proverbially fond of putting vine-leaves or some symbolic substitute for vine-leaves, in their hair. Here I saw the typical village drunkard, a most sincere and earnest drunkard, one who managed to remain drunk all the time. Yet he displayed much of that physical vigor and that cheery kindliness that is so characteristic of the Ainu. Unlike most semibarbarous people, the Ainus seem to welcome the intrusions of the white man. They have no written literature and they have no real religion. They believe in good and evil spirits and they worship bears, perhaps because bears are more hairy than themselves. Every village has its shrine, a bear cage, with a living god, a bear, enshrined therein. They treat the creature like a king, feed him and fatten him, and in due time, with much deliberate and elaborate ceremony, they kill him and eat him, and put another bear into the cage to be fattened for some future festival.

Their huts or houses are unlike the homes of the Japanese. The roofs of reeds are fashioned in layers with considerable skill. They spread mats on the earthen floor, their household utensils are few and crude and simple, and their handicrafts are more advanced than one might well expect. Wood carving they do fairly well and they weave a limited quantity of rather fine brocade.

The dress of the women is very like that of the men, dark blue with bold patterns applied in red and white. When I began distributing the glittering trinkets I had brought as presents, I discovered that the Ainu women, old and young, are swayed by the same desires and cupidities that sway a certain proportion of the sex in other lands. One only, a very young one, refused the proferred bribe. She simply would not pose for her picture even after I had handed her a pretty little pin of which apparently her costume stood in great need. But she was honest—she gave back the pin and fled in tears.

The elders were less finicky. They eagerly accepted

our contribution toward the expenses of their favorite ceremony, for which they had already taken their positions. They awaited only the return of the youngest and spryest of their bewhiskered companions, who had gone on the run to the distant tavern to procure the spirit that was to move this solemn meeting. As soon as it arrived it was poured forth in generous libations, and the feast, the liquid feast, began. Never have I seen such dignified dissipation. Slowly, with deliberate gestures, with almost sacerdotal dignity, the lacquer cups of saké, or rice wine, are lifted in one hand, while with the spatula, a flat blade of wood, held in the other hand, imaginary somethings are lifted from the liquid and tossed lightly in the air. It looks as if they were removing flies or mosquitoes which had fallen in the cup. This was repeated many times, and then the spatula was placed against the upper lip, the long mustache was lifted and held up while slowly the drinker drank the drink, closing his eyes as if in solemn ecstasy, the aged drinkers utterly oblivious to all save the exact and proper doing of the thing that they had set themselves to do. [See colorplate on page 51]

1894   INTO MOROCCO

Nelson and I left the ship at Algiers resolved to see North Africa in our own way, in leisurely fashion, taking time and taking pictures. It was for us a glorious adventure—Algeria, the Kabyle mountains, Biskra and a long slow drive with the *"courier des postes"* to Touggourt far out across the Sahara sands. My skill at sleight-of-hand—and Barnes was not bad at it either—stood us in good stead. We performed for little Arab audiences at the cafés in the towns and outside the adobe houses of the desert villages. Our reputation as wonder-workers spread fast and far from oasis to oasis. At every stop, we were requested to manifest our powers. By the time we got to Touggourt, we had worked up quite a little program of illusions. We would cut a hole in the fine white burnous of a sheik, and while he sat discomfited and fearful of irreparable damage, we would set fire to the edges of the aperture and then with mystic passes and such hocus-pocus, mend the garment perfectly! There would remain no trace of cut or scorching. Card tricks also delighted our easily bamboozled spectators. Arab playing cards are different in design but used much as we use cards in Christian countries. I purchased several packs, careful to have the back-designs all similar so that I could do all the old stunts of forcing a card, persuading the spectator to tear it up, burning the pieces, blowing away the ashes and causing the restored card to be found—intact and scathless in the hood of some bystander's burnous.

Touggourt was then a far outpost of French influence, a town to which came caravans from the depths of the Sahara. By night the vast square between the Spahi barracks and the crude one-story hotel was literally paved with kneeling camels, sleeping camel-drivers and bales of desert merchandise. When morning broke, the rumor of those waking caravans made music such as we had never heard. Soon they were gone. Naught remained but sunshine and silence; sunshine too brilliant, silence too complete.

In the cool of evening, groups of white-clad noble-

looking men gathered at the cafés, neglecting their card games and their dominoes to watch us do our tricks. A small committee waited on our guide, requesting him to take us deeper into the desert to the holy town of Temaçin, where dwelt a very famous Marabout or Moslem saint who was himself possessed of supernatural powers and was a worker of many miracles. He would be happy, they assured us, to meet and entertain such holy men as we, such wonder-workers from the infidel Occident.

This seemed to promise an adventure. We consented to make a pilgrimage to the Zaoüia of that celebrated Saint. On horseback, with our guide atop a donkey, we covered the twenty intervening hot and sandy miles from oasis to oasis. The Marabout, a huge, handsome, full-blooded negro, turbaned and robed in spotless white, stood like a gleaming welcome at the adobe gateway of his town of Temaçin. He spoke a little French. Grandly he led us to the tomb of his sainted grandfather, one of the holiest tombs in all Algeria. We silently saluted the resting place of the eminent one whose bones, like those of Christian saints, had worked and were still working many miracles and were bringing many pilgrims and much profit to the shrine. Thence into the whitewashed "palace" of our host, with its semi-occidentalized air, its tables, chairs, and a tall clock from the Bon Marché of Paris. A huge volume—the French variant of a Sears-Roebuck catalogue, was one of the most highly prized objects on display.

Silently, the respectful domestics of the holy man served an elaborate banquet of Oriental and European food and sprinkled us with rose water from slender silver bottles. When the feast ended, the miracle man of Temaçin bade us perform *our* miracles. To our surprise, our tricks, the kind that schoolboys can do, amazed the Marabout. His eyes opened wider and wider and his deep respirations told of his astonishment.

I found that I had forgotten to bring my Arab playing cards and asked if there were any to be had at the Zaoüia. No, but a servant could get a pack from the village shop. Before they came, I rummaged in my pocket and discovered among my letters one solitary playing card. Making mental note that it was the nine of spades, I slipped it as far as possible under the oil-cloth table-cover as I pretended to adjust it when the servant came to spread an embroidered cloth upon it and to set thereon a beautiful brass tray with sweets and beverages for our further delectation.

In time a purchased deck of cards was brought in with the information that it was the only one to be found in the oasis. I did my card tricks. Barnes did his. They were old timers but ranked high as mystifying novelties in Temaçin. Then, as a climax, I prepared for my grand *coup*. Happily the design on the backs of the new cards was identical with that of my "planted" nine of spades. So, forcing a nine of spades upon my host, I bade him tear it up. He protested that he did not wish to spoil the only deck of cards this side of Touggourt. "After what you have seen, can you still doubt my powers?" He tore the card to bits. We burned the bits. Piously, I gathered the ashes, wrapped them in a bit of paper, stood back from the table and "vanished" the packet, announcing that the card would be found, miraculously restored, on the table-top beneath the various covers.

Our dusky saint expressed his incredulity. He motioned to me and Barnes to stand in the far corners of the room. He waved away the servants and then, he himself removed the tray, the embroidered spread and the oil-cloth cover. There before his eyes was proof of our superior magic! The nine of spades intact! His fine eyes rolled. His deep voice boomed. "You

must be great saints in your own country."

Morocco was no place for the tourist in 1894. It was then, as it had been for centuries, an independent empire, closed to the infidel, without roads, hotels, or Christian comforts, and haughtily regardless of the outer world. Few were the travelers who had ventured far beyond the gates of civilized Tangier. Many were the obstacles raised to guard the sanctity and secrecy of the most fanatically religious country of North Africa.

There was real adventure in our Moroccan journey, though we did not seek it or take it seriously when it touched us. We were shot at as we caravaned away from the sacred city of the Shareef of Wazzan. We thought that a little party was out hunting birds and did not suspect that the game they were after was in the form of Christian Dogs. The hunters were bad shots; the bullets whizzed above our heads and, ignorant and unafraid, we calmly rode away.

Our first day in Fez was spent in seeking a place in which to lay our heads. First to the palace of the Basha, or Governor of the Capital, to present our official letter from Tangier and ask the necessary permission to remain within the walls. His Excellency kept us waiting in the courtyard for several hours, then deigned to designate a house in a remote part of the

◄ In no other place will the traveler see beggars more picturesque than in Tangier. Many are blind, and cannot see that we are dogs of infidels and therefore thank us for our offerings. But those who are not sightless bless us not; even when we give, it is their pious duty to curse and vilify the Christian; the dog of an unbeliever cannot even buy their thanks. Their curses are as picturesque and sometimes as vile as their persons. One of the milder forms of anathema, one hurled at us by this animated crazy-quilt, was "May Allah burn your grandmother."

city as our residence. For it, no charge was to be made; we were guests of the city, unhonored guests, who might be asked to leave town at the pleasure of the Basha. A guest cannot refuse to move on when his host says, "Go!"

Keeping house in Fez was, up to 1894, an experience enjoyed by very, very few "Christian Dogs." That epithet was applied to us many times in the course of our ten-day sojourn in the holy city. As we passed through the streets, we thought at first that an epidemic of coughs and colds was raging in all parts of town. There was intermittent coughing and a barrage of expectoration all along our route. This, we learned, was the customary chorus of welcome that greeted unbelievers. Our infidel presence was supposed to pollute the atmosphere of Islam. Men cleared their throats and spat at the sight of Christian Dogs — we two inoffensive but unwelcome visitors being the dogs. We pretended not to understand and not to resent it. It was a novel experience; we rather enjoyed being the objects of so much picturesque contempt. Superbly dressed Moors in their spotless white robes, noble looking, bearded men evidently of the upper class, would draw aside their draperies lest they be defiled by contact with foreign outcasts.

We remained a day and night in our small abode in Fez before venturing out into the streets. We now cautiously commence a series of expeditions—one cannot call them strolls or promenades—across and round about the town. We descend from the high-lying Garden Region, and enter the ruinous streets of the Medina. We are accompanied by Haj, for without our faithful guide we should soon go astray. We are followed by Kaid Lharbi, our military escort, it being most imprudent for the foreigner to walk abroad unaccompanied by a guard. To photograph in the streets of Fez is difficult to the verge of impossibility. First, there is the Mohammedan prejudice against picture-making, the reproduction of the likeness of living things being prohibited by the Koran.

Even though this difficulty may be overcome by cunning, the very streets conspire with the people to foil the eager camerist. Street life in Fez is vividly suggestive of subterranean existence. There is a dark cellar-like coolness, which, combined with the ghostly stride and costume of the inhabitants, gives us the impression of being in the catacombs among resuscitated men in their shrouds.

Haj, rascal that he is, knowing that I care more for snap-shots than for introductions, always arranges when he meets a friend or relative to detain him in conversation, in the best illuminated portion of the street, thus giving us invaluable opportunities for secret portraiture. Then, after he has heard the "click!" that comes from what appears to be an innocent brown paper parcel under my right arm, Haj, with many complimentary phrases, presents us to our visitor, introducing us as men of great distinction from America.

But as for the ladies we encountered—bless their feminine souls!—with them, womanly curiosity proved stronger than religious prejudice. They frankly halted as we passed, turned their pretty faces toward us and gazed up smilingly at the arriving travelers. We must admit, however, that they had the advantage of us; we were compelled to take for granted both the prettiness and smiles, and it was pleasanter to do so; moreover, there was nothing else to do. Still, the features of her who paused on the left, as vaguely molded by the masking haik, were not of Grecian purity. She would have charmed us more had she not drawn her veil so tight. On the right an older woman was more discreet; like the wise Katisha she

believed that it is not alone in the face that beauty is to be sought, so she sparingly displayed her charms, revealing only a left heel which people may have come many miles to see. The fair one in the middle bares her face in a most immodest fashion: through an opening at least three quarters of an inch in width two pretty eyes of black are flaming; and indeed, it may be set down as an almost invariable rule that the wider the opening 'twixt veil and haik, the prettier the eyes that flash between.

We have now approached a portion of the Beni Hasan territory, a region inhabited by a tribe whose chief pursuit is robbery, whose supreme joy is murder; and the placing of a guard around the tent is no longer a mere formality. As yet, however, we have seen no roving bands; but next day as we file across the flower-spotted plain, we observe on the horizon a number of moving patches of bright color. With lighning-like rapidity, these flashes of color sweep toward us, each one resolving itself into a Moorish cavalier, well mounted, fully armed, and seemingly upon the lookout for adventure. These, then, are Beni Hasan men! What will they do to us and how shall we greet them? is our anxious thought, as they draw nearer, brandishing their rifles, shouting as they ride. The first brief moment of alarm is, however, quickly ended. The chief salutes us cordially; asks Haj whence we come, whither we are going; and then, desirous of showing honor to us (for he looked upon foreign travelers as great men of distinction), he offers to perform for us a fantasia. A fantasia is an exhibition of Arabian horsemanship, a sort of glorified cavalry-charge, a spectacular maneuver, the favorite amusement of the Moorish cavalier, the exercise in which he takes most pleasure and most pride.

A dozen cavaliers, each one a savage, long-haired son of Hasan, advance across the plain, their horses aligned breast with breast. They twirl aloft their richly inlaid guns; then, putting their chargers to their fullest speed, the riders rise in the stirrups, seize the reins between their teeth, and sweep toward us in swift majesty. On go the horses at full gallop, still accurately in line. Faster and faster spin the guns above the riders' heads; now muskets are tossed high in air, and descending are caught by strong bronzed hands that never fail. On go the horses; then the men, still standing in the stirrups, their loose garments enveloping them like rapid-flying clouds, at a signal discharge a rousing volley, and under cover of the smoke, check—almost instantaneously with the cruel bits—their panting horses bloody-mouthed and deeply scarred and wounded by the spurs.

The Fantasia, Morocco, 1894.

Mount Fuji in winter, 1892.

Ainu villagers, 1892.

The Crystal Palace, 1897.

Punting on the Thames, 1897.

A street scene in London, 1897.

The White City of the Esplanade, with Napoleon's Tomb in the background. Universal Exposition, Paris, 1900.

The manned balloon, one of the most spectacular sights at the Universal Exposition of Paris, 1900.

1895 PARIS

Who can resist the charm of Paris? I confess that I cannot. To me it is a pleasure simply to be in Paris. With every recurring visit, I find that I gaze on it with a sense of novelty, an interest and a pleasure for which I can find no expression in words.

There is no place in all the world like Paris. No city charms and fascinates us like the city by the Seine.

None of the world's capitals is so truly the capital of the great world.

The boisterous fountains strive, vainly or successfully, ▼ according to our mood, to teach forgetfulness of the inevitable, and seem to sing that Paris, having been, will ever be. The ones at the left are at Versailles.

An almost incredible train accident at the Montparnasse Railroad Station.

The Rue de l'Opéra.

A street market with clothing peddlers.

Whoever you may be, whatever things attract you, you will be at home in Paris; you will find there the very thing you seek—Paris is all things to all men.

1896 VENICE

Venice is still victorious over Time. Despite her age, the City of the Sea is fascinating still. She has successfully defied a dozen centuries; she may well defy as many more. All other cities in the world resemble one another. Venice remains unique. She is the City of Romance—the only place on earth today where Poetry conquers Prose.

The Rialto Bridge remains a relic of Venice in her ▶ glory, for its huge arch is entirely of marble, and has a length of over a hundred and fifty feet. Its cost exceeded half a million dollars; and the foundations, which for three hundred and twenty years have faithfully supported it, are twelve thousand trunks of elm trees, each ten feet in length....

Wave before it, for an instant, the magic wand of fancy and we can picture to ourselves how it must have looked when on this Rivo-Alto, or "High Bank," which gives the bridge its name, Venetian ladies saw outspread before them the treasures of the orient; when at this point the laws of the Republic were proclaimed; when merchants congregated here as to a vast Exchange; and when, on this same bridge, the forms of Shylock and Othello may have stood out in sharp relief against the sky.

YELLOWSTONE PARK

Late in the sixties the attention of the world was directed to an unexplored region in the northwestern corner of Wyoming.

Strange rumors had been set afloat concerning the existence there among the Rockies, near the headwaters of a river called the Yellowstone, of an almost

inaccessible plateau, where mysterious phenomena of a most startling character were grouped as in an enchanted amphitheater.

Accordingly, a number of exploring parties were sent out to confirm or to disprove the extravagant statements that had long been rife. When the leaders of these expeditions, on their return to civilization, submitted their reports, these were at first received incredulously; the world would not believe that wonders such as they described existed elsewhere than in the imagination of the daring travelers. It was soon proved that a new Wonderland had been discovered;

and Congress, acting with commendable promptitude, decreed that this territory where Nature had assembled so many of her marvelous creations, this land she had so long shrouded in mystery, should be set apart as a perpetual playground for the Nation.

What traveler to Yellowstone does not remember Larry Matthews and his canvas palace? Who can forget his cheery welcome when, lifting the ladies from the coach, he cried: "Glad to see you! Walk right upstairs—or would ye rather take the elevator?" His ready wit is remarkable. Every day he is expected to be funny from 11 to 2 o'clock, during which hours he must not only delight the inbound tourists, but carefully avoid repeating himself in the presence of those outward bound who lunch for the second time. . . .

It was at Larry's that I met the original Simon-pure ▶ "Calamity Jane," who twenty years ago was famous as a woman scout and served our generals faithfully in many of the Indian wars.

1897 ROUND ABOUT LONDON

London is the most important place on earth. It is not only the most populous, it is the greatest of great cities. No other city is the center of so many world-wide interests. Toward no other city do so many human beings look for inspiration, for commands, and for reward. London is splendidly unbeautiful; its architecture, for the most part, grandly ungraceful; its walls covered with a cleanly grime. London is leisurely animated; it roars in a gentle monotone that to American ears, hardened to the clattering thunder of our streets, seems almost quietude or silence.

When in London one should take at least one hansom, ▶ if only to admire the marvelous skill of London cab drivers in winding through the throngs of vehicles and pedestrians which surge through the narrow streets and bridges. It is probably the peculiar position from which a hansom cabby looks upon the hubs of his own and his neighbors' wheels that enables him to estimate to almost a hair's breadth the space required for him to pass; but nothing I have ever seen in any other portion of the world can equal the ability thus displayed. [See also colorplate on page 54]

A popular resort for London's multitudes is at Sydenham, eight miles from London, where the famous Crystal Palace looms grandly, like a colossal bubble curiously shaped. The great glass house is more than sixteen hundred feet in length, and its nave one hundred and seventy-five feet high. The glass and iron that enter into its construction were first used in the building of the first great Industrial Expo held in Hyde Park in 1851. This Crystal Palace commemorates the opening of the epoch of those colossal industrial shows that we now call World's Fairs. [See colorplate page 52]

◄ Summer in England is a season of delight and the River Thames is the scene of the most delightful doings of that season.

The greatest of great days on the River comes with the Henley Regatta early in July, when all of fashionable England seems to gather on the River. Then the Thames presents an astounding picture, glorious in color, scintillating with the sunshine of bright skies, bright eyes, and the glint of flashing oars and paddles. There are of course boat races to give a special thrill of excitement from hour to hour—but all day long we may enjoy the quiet, joyous, lasting thrill born of this pleasing picture of the very pleasant life lived by nature-loving pleasure-seekers who seek and find real pleasure on their best-beloved River. [See also colorplate on page 52-53]

1898 HAWAII

The first impressions of the traveler, as he sees the islands rise like pale blue clouds out of the dark blue sea, I shall not endeavor to describe. I trust that all of you are some day going to the islands, and believe no one has a right to rob you of your first impressions.

Pearl Harbor is famous in Hawaii; but it has, as we know, a wider fame, as the only available site for a naval station in all that vast watery desert between California and Asia, between Alaska and the Antarctic seas. It is not only the sole safe harbor of Hawaii, it is as perfectly adapted to the needs of a modern naval power as if it had been planned and dredged and blasted out by naval engineers.

The water is from five to ten fathoms deep; in many places men-of-war could be moored immediately alongside the coral bluffs in seven fathoms of clear water. No hurricanes can reach this haven, no malaria broods upon the shores by night; there is abundant water from artesian wells, and Honolulu is but twenty minutes distant by the railway. The removal of a sandbar, a very simple proposition, will transform these almost virgin waters into the grandest, safest, and most attractive harbor in the world.

Nature apparently foresaw the destiny of these Pearl Lochs, for she has wisely built a coral belt two and one-half miles wide between the inner lochs and the sea; then to prevent the landing of an enemy—to force an attacking fleet to abandon strategy, to compel it to transact its business at the fortified front-door, she has concealed beneath the fawning breakers, far out at sea, a deadly coral reef, which may be passed only by ships that steer directly for the harbor entrance.

As we walk about the island, we cannot but fear that the leisure-loving native is doomed. He flourished like the vegetation of his island so long as he was left to grow his taro, pick his mango, and idly repose. There was no necessity for labor. Then the white man came with his doctrine of activity, whereupon for the first time the

curse of Cain descended on this happy land. The islander did not resist; one by one he simply laid him down to die; he will revenge himself by disappearing from the earth where he no longer feels at home.

This young girl is Princess Kaiulani, to whom annexation by the United States means the abandonment of hope, the end of her dreams of royalty. As it is, she is queen in the hearts of many, although her disappointments and sorrows have tinged her character with just a shade of bitterness, for it is difficult to be resigned to a career so different from that which fortune promised. ▶

In 1899 America was looking with anxious interest toward the Philippines. Admiral Dewey, his work accomplished, had left Manila; General Otis, as military governor, was in command; the Filipinos under Aguinaldo were successfully defending themselves, and all the American forces were confined to the immediate surroundings of Manila and to a thin wedge of country bordering the railway that leads northward from the capital.

This being the situation, it would appear that little inducement was offered to the traveler to direct his steps toward the Far Eastern archipelago that fate had assigned to Uncle Sam. But Manila itself was accessible, and the situation, political and military, presented picturesque aspects that appealed even to the globetrotter intent only upon what is called in the east a "Look See."

The town of Baliuag is as calm and peaceful as if war was a thing undreamed of. I spend a quiet evening at American headquarters, a fine old dwelling, formerly the home of a rich citizen, which only a few months before had been occupied by Aguinaldo. The insurgents hoped to hold Baliuag. They had constructed wonderful intrenchments along the road leading toward the railway. They felt secure; but the Americans, instead of fighting their way past line after line of trenches and fortifications, merely changed their plans, marched around behind the town, and then walked calmly in through the back door, while Aguinaldo and his Filipinos fled so hurriedly that they had not time to set fire to the place. Hence Baliuag is the most comfortable post along our line. It is intact, and every officer has decent quarters. The men are quartered in the church—a splendid barracks, spacious, clean and elaborately decorated. Throughout the island churches are used both as barracks and forts. They are usually solid structures, capable of being easily defended. But every Sunday the church at Baliuag is cleared while an American priest, chaplain of the regiment, officiates at the high altar, in the presence of the native population.

THE TRAVELER'S HEYDAY

1900–1914

The first fourteen years of the twentieth century were wonderful years for the traveler, especially for one who was intent on photographing the life and customs of foreign countries. There were then very few who carried cameras and everybody was willing and even eager to help the picture-maker. The world was mine for those happy years. I was almost alone in the then peculiar field of showing Americans what the world, outside of America, looked like.

◄ There is a "Quiet Paris" full of serenity and calm. This peaceful Paris is not a special quarter; it is made up of many and various fragments scattered far and wide.

The street that leads from the Place Vendôme to the ► Opéra is the celebrated Rue de la Paix, the street dear to the heart of the American woman and dearer to the purse of her indulgent husband. It's lots of fun to go out shopping with Americans in Paris, especially when with someone who really means to order several gowns. The fashionable dressmaking establishments make it pleasant for the men who traipse along; the women of course find pleasure in looking at the frocks; the men find even more in looking at the pretty living models or mannequins upon whose shapely forms the new frocks are displayed. These stately show-girls sweep into the salon with the air of uncrowned Empresses, oblivious to the humble would-be purchasers of the finery, which usually becomes the poor but pretty mannequin much better than it does the purse-proud customer. Mere man, of course, will be inclined to pity the poor girls—condemned to strut all day in costly finery that becomes them so well, yet never can become their own. But apparently no pangs of jealousy are felt, even by the less lovely demoiselle who takes my lady's measure so deftly and, as it seems, so carelessly. We men cannot understand how the gowns ever can be made to fit, but here we realize we are getting beyond our depth, and we prudently withdraw.

We stand upon the threshold of the Age of Electricity— ► the Age of Light.

The Universal Exposition of Paris commemorates the close of the nineteenth century, the Age of Steam. And as we look by night upon the Wonder-City of

1900, we see the Eiffel Tower, ablaze with electrical incandescence, pointing like a prophetic finger toward a radiant future—a future in which the Light of Science and the Light of Knowledge shall be universal—a future which shall have no darkness upon the earth, nor shadows in the lives of men.

Shop girls pose for the camera.

1901 RUSSIA

No foreigner can look at Moscow without deep emotion; and as for Russian peasants, when they approach this sacred city of the empire, and see its gilded turrets gleam like golden helmets in the sun, they often fall upon their knees and weep for joy, moved to an ecstasy of religious feeling.

The famous "Red Square" flanks the Kremlin's deeply tinted walls. Its history proves it to have been well named; for, if its pavement could bear witness to the dreadful deeds enacted here, it would be red with blood. Two hundred years ago, this was the place of public punishment, and victims were treated with horrible brutality.

The home of Count Tolstoi in Moscow is an unpretentious dwelling, to which we sent our guide one day to ask if the Count would see us if we should call. The servants told the guide that the Count was out. He was; for as our emissary turned away, he saw the aged writer issuing from another door to take a carriage. In a very few words he stated his mission. The Count replied in this oracular fashion: "I am not at home to all the world; above all I am not at home for interviews; but an American can always find me."

But to find Count Tolstoi is, even for an American, a thing easier said than done; for before we could accept the invitation, or challenge, to seek him out, he had left Moscow and retired to his country seat, Yasnaya Polyana, near the town of Tula. But, not discouraged, we gladly undertook a six-hour railway journey to Tula, and a carriage-drive of fifteen versts to the estate of the "grand old man" of Russia.

We arrived at half-past eight in the morning; for believing that Count Tolstoi, despite his great age, seventy-two years, was still leading the life of a peasant farmer, we thought the hour none too early. But no one was astir except a servant. We wait for an hour and a half, driving through the adjacent village, peopled by the folk whose fathers were the serfs of the Tolstoi estate. Rank misery pervades the filthy and disgusting village-settlement, no better and no worse than villages in other parts of Russia.

A deformed woman and a big strapping mujik are insistent in their demands for money, and servile in their thanks upon receiving it. As we gaze about us, we strive in vain to reconcile the altruistic theories of the master and the existent conditions in this village at his gates.

At ten o'clock we again present ourselves at the Count's door. His eldest son, who bears the father's name, receives us kindly with the words, "Father will be here presently." Meantime we have observed, beneath a tree near the door, three peasant women waiting patiently; they were waiting there when we first came, two hours earlier. At last they seem to wake; they rise expectantly as an old man in mujik costume steps briskly down from the veranda. It is Count Leo Tolstoi, one of the world's great men.

A hurried greeting to us, a fatherly smile to Leo, Jr., and the Count begs our indulgence for a moment, saying as he turns toward the old peasant women under the tree, "You must excuse me. These poor women first. They have had a fire in their village; three

◀ An impressive sight is the Tsar of Bells, the hugest in the world, weighing two hundred tons. The bell was cast in 1735, but was not taken from the mold until two years later, before which time, unhappily, a conflagration cracked off a fragment nearly seven feet in height, and robbed the mighty bronze of the deep voice that might have been today one of the supreme sound sensations of the world.

That broken hulk has a fascination for every passer-by; it is worn glossy by the touch of sympathetic hands, which every day caress it curiously. No one seems able to resist the attraction of this magnet—warmed by the sun, it offers to every touch an almost human contact, as if a little of the life of all the millions who have fondled it had in some mysterious way passed into this mass of bronze and made of it a sentient, responsive thing.

times they have had a fire; they have lost many things and I must speak to them." It is all perfectly sincere and beautiful; but—cynics that we are—we think how marvelously effective it all is from the dramatic point of view: The waiting pensioners beneath the ancestral tree; the aged lord of the manor, who, though a nobleman, is clad in the dress of the poor mujik, hastily courteous to his foreign guests, but most concerned with the misfortunes of the native poor who await him.

Tolstoi speaks English fluently, but with an accent that suggests the speech of Henry Irving, with an added Gallic twist. He talks upon a dozen subjects with equal interest, enthusiasm, and, above all, originality. There should be no law; no man should have the right to judge or to condemn another; absolute freedom of the individual is the only thing that will redeem the world. Christ was a great teacher, nothing more. This was the sum and substance of his views as expressed to us in June, 1901. But Tolstoi both claims and exercises the right to revise opinions, and proclaims from time to time a new and always startling attitude toward the truths and contentions in the great area of philosophic thought.

We breakfasted with him on the veranda, a large and loving family gathered round the samovar; the two dainty grandchildren relieved with a note of youth and hope and freshness the almost sad impression produced upon us by the atmosphere of neglect and tumbledownness permeating not only the peasant village but even the house and private grounds of the estate, of which the Russian title, "Yasnaya Polyana," means the Bright Plain, or the Illuminated Field. Even if we cannot sympathize with the almost fatalistic philosophy of a return to nature—a philosophy that would let all things return to seed, we are not blind to the brightness that illuminates Yasnaya Poliana, for it is the brightness of a mighty mind, an intellectual luminosity that has lighted for all time the dark path trodden by oppressed humanity.

One of the most potent instruments of world-dominion today is the railway. Russia wields many modern weapons. The Trans-Siberian Railway is the latest acquisition in her arsenal of conquest. The Moscow terminal station may be regarded not only as the gateway to Siberia, but also as the gateway to the Orient, for it will soon be possible to travel in through-trains from that station to Peking.

Those who, pursuing the New Way Around the World, journey from Moscow to the eastern edge of Asia, can trace the orbit of this east-bound Star of Empire, the star of the inevitable Muscovite, who, in his turn, despite the checks and the defeats that may become his portion, is destined to play a dominant part in the great world-drama of the future.

On the 19th of June, 1901, we begin our nine days' journey toward the Rising Sun. For three days we roll on across the somber lands of eastern Russia, where there is little to relieve the sad monotony save the crossing of several rivers and glimpses of big ragged cities on the Volga. But that which will linger longest in my memory is the hopeless aspect of the Russian villages, which look like groups of haystacks or of mounds of refuse. I cannot at first believe that the shapeless heaps scattered around one or two frame houses and a modest church are the abodes of human beings. But in these congeries of hovels we touch the very depths of Russian misery; as we leave the old overworked acres of Europe behind us, the condition of the people and the aspect of their housing steadily improves.

We are impressed by the thought that for nine days the endless panorama of Siberia is to unroll itself to us as we stand gazing from the windows of our car. I say "stand" gazing because that is what we did all day and day after day in the confined space of the narrow corridor of our sleeping-car. The train is one of the Trains d'État, or Government Trains. It is composed of five long carriages, one first-class, two second-class, one restaurant- and one baggage-car. The compartment was comfortable, the crude and ill-kept public washrooms the only objectionable feature. The fare from Moscow to Irkutsk was a little less than fifty dollars.

The dining car is a stuffy little affair with a piano at one end and a bookcase at the other—but neither music nor literature appeared to appeal to the passengers, for the ivories remained untouched and the books undisturbed. The meals, though badly served, were surprisingly well-cooked and appetizing; good bread, excellent veal, and hearty soups, steaming hot, with a hunk of beef rising from them like a volcanic island, and sometimes frappés, with a clinking cake of ice floating on their chilly depths.

Meals as cheap as they are satisfying may be had in the station restaurant, and as for the untidiness of the service, we have been too long in Russia to take note of it. As a cure for squeamishness let me prescribe a period of Russian travel. For example, napkins are rarely washed; the patrons carelessly throw them down; the waiters pick them up from the floor and chair and table, spread them out as flat as possible, spray them with water, fold them very carefully, and then put them in presses, so that at next meal-time they may be again produced with neat new creases that deceive those who have never chanced to look behind the scenes.

There is not much to photograph along the way. But rarely do we get away from any of the stations without the customary interview with the police and military guards. As courteous as in Russia, and even more strict in the performance of their duties, the watchful officers, at sight of cameras in foreign hands, invariably demand by virtue of what official paper the camera is being used. The letter given us by Prince Khilkoff, the Minister of Railways, proves a most potent "Boumaga," and that august document is continually produced and is very respectfully perused by the police at almost every station that lies between the Baltic and the Japan Sea.

Departures are announced by the ringing of a big bell at the station. We soon learn not to be startled by the first ring, for it means merely that it is time to begin to think about beginning to commence to get ready to prepare to go. By and by comes another clap or two, just to remind us that the bell has rung before. Then finally, after we have stepped aboard at the polite personal request of the numerous employees, a final ultimate and authoritative clang announces that some-

thing is really going to happen, by and by.

Sure enough, after a shrill blast from the whistle of the station-master, a toot from the horn of the switchman, and a squeak from the locomotive, the Trans-Siberian Flyer does move at last and before long there is nothing in sight except distance, bisected by the straight and seemingly endless line of the track.

Thus we speed eastward for many hundreds of miles across a Dakota-like expanse. There is little variety in the landscape, one day all plain, another day all marsh, another day nothing but endless curvings in tree-bordered aisles, where the sense of vastness takes possession of us.

On the ninth evening we roll into the great Siberian city of Irkutsk—metropolis of northern Asia. We are

on time to the minute; but this is not remarkable, for the schedule is so arranged that if the brakes were not in working order, even these leisurely, inexperienced trains would have difficulty in avoiding premature arrivals. We have covered roughly three thousand miles—between Moscow and Irkutsk—in nine days, at an average speed of about fifteen miles an hour.

Irkutsk is a wilderness of mud; it appears almost magnificent as one views it from a church tower, but disillusion awaits the traveler below. I cannot understand why photographs should make the city look so trim when in reality it is so soiled and dingy and unkempt.

Russia is always striving for effect, and here in Irkutsk we get the same impression as in St. Petersburg, of a city built to order—designed to impress the observer. The same "stone" walls of stucco, the same "marble" pillars of staff, the wide streets and the endless avenues, still unpaved and insistently suggestive of

83

the wilderness of which they lately formed a part. Space is the cheapest thing in northern Asia. The Russians have been prodigal of space in laying out their cities. The Orthodox Cathedral is huge enough to satisfy the needs of a city four times the present size of Irkutsk; but the critical tourist must not forget that Irkutsk will in the near future quadruple its population.

We board another train eastward from the busy, crowded station of Irkutsk, continuing our journey to Lake Baikal. The railway around the mountainous south shore of the lake will not be finished before 1905, because of the alpine nature of the country; therefore we must now quit the train and hasten to embark on the ice-breaking ferry-boat. We boarded the Trans-Baikal train at Myssovaya. After a four-day journey from Irkutsk, we arrived at Stryetensk on the Shilka River, the Trans-Siberian terminal, in July, 1901. Our trip was to be continued down the Shilka River to the Amur, and thence along the Amur's banks to Khabarovsk. Before the completion of the railway, the tide of travel was still flowing down the waterways. As we soon discover, it is not flowing easily—there is both a boat- and a water-famine on the river. There is very little water in the shallow Shilka, horse carts may cross it with ease, but as a result of the shallowness, no boats are in port. The post-boat steamer had left the day before our arrival, carrying our friends who had not lingered in Irkutsk but had hastened on to make sure of the official steamer. We had taken our chances on catching it, and had lost the steamer.

Our ferry crossing of the Shilka the night of our arrival was an unforgettable experience. Sitting on top of our innumerable bags and boxes, piled high on two barbaric wagons, we were whirled down a steep embankment, then out into the river, the water rising to the wagon-floor, then up a steep incline to the deck of an overcrowded barge, which slowly swung part way

across the stream, and there discharged its cargo, the horse and wagons splashing through the shallows, and jolting over submerged boulders until the shore is gained. Experienced by day all this may be amusing; but in the pitchy darkness of a stormy night when one cannot see ten feet ahead, it is, to tired travelers, an ordeal most terrifying. We secured miserable accommodations in the pretentious hotel called the Star of the Orient. "Disgusting" is the adjective most generally applicable to the Siberian hotels.

The next day we celebrated the glorious Fourth of July with a noon-day banquet of American dishes cooked by our ambitious amateur chef and washed down with three bottles of the beverage that makes Milwaukee famous. We are exactly on the other side of the world. We realize that we are as far away from home as we can get, that we have reached the half-way point of our journey at the forsaken, boatless river-port of Stryetensk; and to our discouraged minds the prospects are that we shall be compelled to stay in this place forever.

We see around us many other travelers stranded here at Stryetensk, for it is the season of low water. There are "officially assisted" settlers, and other emigrants, poorer and more independent, camping along the dirty waterfront waiting for the steamer, of which the arrival is as uncertain as is the possibility of a subsequent departure, for the river is falling rapidly.

We saw lying near the steamer-landing a despairing female who had given up the whole affair as a bad piece of business, and had fallen back on her reserve supply of vodka as the surest ship to the harbors of forgetfulness. For three days that miserable creature lay there in a stupor, unmolested save by the chilling rain of one night and the burning sun of the ensuing day. Now and then she would wake, take a long pull at the bottle that she gripped tightly even while she lay unconscious, and then, with a glassy stare at the empty, receding river, resume her horrid revery.

But just as our stay in Stryetensk threatens to become a waking nightmare—the dirt, the heat, the discomfort and uncertainty beginning to get on our nerves—our Russian friend makes a glorious discovery. He rushes over to report that the good ship "Rurik," drawing only two feet of water, has been reclaimed from some fluvial bone-yard and hastily thrown into shape to take advantage of the extraordinary conditions that prevail during the summer of 1901.

CHINA

Peking, capital of the Celestial Empire—fortified camp of the Manchu conquerors—acres of dead magnificence and living desolation, half hidden in a glorifying haze of incandescent dust—dominated by sixteen towering city gates—shut in by miles of jealous walls now breached and tunneled for the invading locomotive—the troops of many nations quartered in her sacred places—her innermost, "Forbidden City" become the playground of the curious—the palaces of the absent "Son of Heaven" profaned and despoiled of their empty mysteries—her population cowed and embittered, regarding with mute defiance the exodus of the avengers and the rebuilding of the fortress-like legations—this is the Peking of the year of Our Lord 1901.

Impression-gathering in the Peking streets is a delightful occupation. I cannot conceive of anybody being bored in Peking. For him who has eyes to see and ears to hear and a nose to smell there is, in the language of the continuous vaudeville advertisements, "something doing every minute." The common, continuous passing throng is in itself enough to hold the attention for hours at a time; and to vary its marvelous monotony of brown body, blue trousers, and upheld paper fan, there are the vehicles, of many sorts—the low carts laden high with military supplies, drawn by small ponies, driven by half-nude teamsters; the familiar, but ever-astonishing passenger-cart, with its blue arched roof, its taut-stretched awning shielding mule and driver; the frail jinrikishas, modern competitors of the perennial carts, with their unhappy passengers, swaying and clutching at nothing as the bare-torsoed runners pull and propel the quivering vehicle over the rutted granite blocks and through the abysmal puddles; the loud-voiced native wheelbarrows, squealing their woeful song, uttering the mortal complaint of the poor dumb human brutes who push them:—all these things go by as we stand watching and watching beneath one of those strange street arches known as "pailows," memorial structures erected in honor of some great or good personage of whom we never heard. [See plate on page 86]

—————

◄ Quaintness, beauty, and wonder are everywhere combined; witness the curious Imperial barge of marble, graceful in outline, and marvelous because it seems to float as lightly as a craft of wood upon the lovely artificial lake. Above, are grouped pagodas, temples, shrines, and summer houses. Below, their tinted forms are mirrored in the blue; and just astern of the white marble marvel is a bridge with curving roofs of tile, unique in form, rich in color, and exquisite in workmanship.

The junk, we are told, was the peace-offering of a corrupt naval official, who, discovered in diverting appropriations for the building of ships into his private pocket, built for the forgiving Emperor an ever-lasting ship on board of which the Son of Heaven could forget his cares, and, incidentally, the roguery of his officials.

—————

We have already seen the Peking of the miserable ▼ many, formerly the only Peking known to the alien intruder. We are now to see the once invisible Peking of the "Son of Heaven," the Peking of the Celestial princes and imperial ministers—the Peking of the privileged and semi-sacred few. Peking is planned upon a grander scale than any of the world's great capitals. Peking has developed within the rigid limita-

tions of a plan designed to emphasize the inviolability and sanctity and glory of the Imperial Person.

Until the foreign invaders in 1901 broke down the barriers of tradition and penetrated to the very heart of this unseen city, it was one of the world's mysteries, guarded by the world's most wonderful walls.

──────────

◄ This Great Wall was begun seventeen hundred years before Columbus discovered America! Before any of the great nations of Europe had come into existence. It is even today a mute reminder of the splendid civilization the Chinese must have had in the long ago days, when our own ancestors were living in huts and sleeping on straw.

──────────

A short distance from Peking in the countryside we ▲ approach the object of our outing, the Summer Palace of the Emperor of China. "Oriental," "fanciful," "curious," or "impossible," carry not half enough of meaning to reveal the wondrously strange charm of this world-famous site.

We set out to climb the famous Hill of Ten Thousand Ages, covered like the Palatine at Rome with palaces and temples. But how unlike the Roman piles are these unheard-of architectural forms! How fascinatingly foreign to the art we inherit are the designs, the coloring, the noble ensemble, and the naive details. Confused by the multiplicity of stairways, terraced courts, and winding paths, I cannot see how best to reach the height that is our goal.

91

aspect. But where could we find hills richer in pleasing lines, greener in summer verdure, than the heights which rear themselves there in the west to shelter Peking from the cruel winds of the adjacent Gobi Desert.

◄ The clothes I saw in China were all rather somber in color, and very severe in effect. The children, to be sure, wear gay colors and patterns, and in the summer hardly bother with clothes at all, or those that are worn are well-ventilated.

A cruel thralldom it is, that of Chinese tradition. One ► of the most painful proofs is—the martyred feet of Chinese women. Revolting to the foreign eye, the so-called "Lily Feet" are deemed both beautiful and fashionable by four hundred million Asiatics. What matter the sufferings of the child?—her baby feet wrapped in the crippling bandages during the years of growth—bandages that are folded tighter month by month as the violated little foot strives to assert its rights to live and grow—making childhood one long martyrdom of intense, never-remitting agony? What matter the inability of the crippled woman to move without a twinge of pain? She is a Chinese woman, and Chinese women must have "Lily Feet." The very walk of the Lily Footed lady—a stilted, uncertain toddle—betrays the suffering resulting from a simple promenade. Some cannot walk at all without a cane. And in this cruel custom China persists, despite the good example set by her sisters of the Manchu race, the wives and daughters of the conquering Mongols who subjugated China three centuries ago, imposed the pigtail on the men, but did not take the bindings from the feet of women.

Breathless with admiration and with exertion, we climb the countless steps that lead up through this architectural wonderland, until we reach the topmost floor of the pagoda. There what little breath remains is taken from us as our gaze leaps out across the lake and lights upon the dainty little island linked by a dainty bridge to the green fertile shore. The beauty of the scene surprises us. We pictured China as an ugly land—a land of graceless shapes and of forbidding

◄ Shanghai is the great commercial port of central China, situated on a river that empties into the estuary of the Yangtze-Kiang. The region here is a flat mud plain, and the city is as flat and ugly and hustling as are many of the cities of our own western plains. Indeed, except in a few minor ways, a man from Chicago or Detroit or Omaha feels quite at home in Shanghai.

Nothing I have seen in foreign ports has prepared me ► for the arrival at Canton. At first glance the city repels, and at the same time fascinates. Our approach is the signal for squadrons of sampans to form in line of battle. Each craft is crowded with half-naked natives gesticulating wildly in their efforts to attract the attention of the Chinese passengers whom they are eager to serve either as porters or as boatmen.

Ofttimes these reckless sampan people meet with disaster; their boats are frequently crushed or overturned by the advancing steamer, and the crews mangled by the propellers or paddles. But these little mishaps create scarce a ripple of dismay, and no regret whatever—there are too many sampans in the Canton River and many more poverty-stricken boat folk dependent on this traffic—a sampan less means a score less of competitors.

KOREA

Strong are the bonds that bind the Koreans to customs of the past. No man may wear the horsehair hat until he has acquired a top-knot, and no man may do his hair up in a top-knot until he has announced his intention to wed.

Korea is indeed the land of hats, and every hat has its significance. But where did that curious cone of horsehair, so delicate, so inconvenient, and so picturesque come from. Like all things interesting it is the result of evolution. Once upon a time, for the story goes back a long way, to the days of feudal strife, of clashing clans. A very wise king of the time hit upon a plan to tame his quarrelsome lords and princes and place a check upon conspiracies. "If men cannot put their heads together, they cannot conspire," said this king; "therefore, my lords, you must wear hats so big that you will have to shout at each other." He prescribed the size and shape of hats for all his subjects, and made the constant wearing of the hat obligatory. The removal of it was regarded as an act of treason; injury to the hat brought deep disgrace upon the wearer. Thus fighting and conspiracy were snuffed out by those hats so large, men could not converse save in loud tones, and dared not fight because the hat was made of pottery, and a broken hat meant a broken fortune at court. Times changed, and the Korean hat began its evolution, and finally the fantastic fly-traps of today emerged triumphant in their elegance and comfort, with which are still combined some of the essential bigness and breakability.

◄ I see comparatively few women in the streets of Seoul. Most of them are shrouded in coats of brilliant green, which are not put on like coats, but merely thrown over the head and clutched under the chin, concealing the faces as do the veils and haiks of Moorish women. The sleeves which dangle free and empty have white cuffs, while long red ribbons add a dash of brilliancy to this striking costume. The coat, however, is not supposed to be the woman's own; despite its use by married women in general, the fiction has it that it is the fighting costume of the hus-band, which the faithful wife wears in time of peace—never daring to get comfortably into it in the ordinary way for fear that in case of sudden alarm there might be some delay in throwing it upon her valiant spouse as he rushes forth to battle. The red ribbons are supposed to have been stained with the blood of enemies wiped from a dripping sword.

High-ranking officers of the Korean military dress in ▼ such elaborate costumes that they have to be wheeled to battle areas on palanquins.

1902 MADEIRA

At first light our ship entered the harbor of Funchal, the chief town on the beautiful semi-tropical island of Madeira. It is a unique place. Nowhere else can the traveler go sleigh riding under a summery sun over snowless roads. The pebbly pavement is very slippery—the streets are paved, as it were, with ball bearings that do not revolve but do permit the runners of tropic sleds to slide quite freely over them. We make our way to the lower town of Funchal in a hanging garden surrounded by the ocean and the sky and embellished by all that art and nature can contrive to charm the eye. They say that Funchal is a favorite health resort much frequented by convalescents. I should be tempted never to get quite well enough to leave if ever I were sent here to regain my health. Why! It would be enough to make me ill to think of leaving such a place—a place so perfectly adapted to the habits of the human mollusk or the "malade imaginaire." Why get well enough to walk when the hammock bearers need the money so? Up and down steep shady paths they carry you—it is like skimming the soft slopes of Paradise at a lazy loitering pace in a perfectly comfortable and absolutely dependable aeroplane.

LISBON

After a wayworn trip our journey ended abruptly at last when the train, after passing beneath the great aqueduct of Lisbon, plunges into a tunnel, roars along beneath the city and discharges its passengers at a splendid station in the very heart of Lisbon at the depressing hour of five A.M. But two passengers I know of were not to be discharged. A German traveler and myself had slumbered soundly all the night, having put out the feeble lamp in our compartment; the train arrived, no one paid any attention to the un-

This statue of King João I of Portugal stands in the ▼ main square of central Lisbon on the banks of the Tejo; Englishmen named the square after the statue, "Black Horse Square."

lighted carriage, which with its unconscious occupants was about to be shunted back through the tunnel, when an Anglo-Teutonic chorus of protest from the sleepers, awakened by the bumping, surprised the Portuguese officials, who whistled to the engineer to stop the train, and then helped two collarless and coatless foreigners to tumble themselves and their belongings out on the platform, dazed, dreamy, and worst of all quite dumb, for my recently acquired Portuguese had utterly forsaken me.

DENMARK

There were few motorcars in Denmark in 1902. Ours was a French automobile of a very rakish cut, complete with a tall, handsome military chauffeur, both belonging to a colonel in the Danish army who placed them at our disposal for a tour. But wonderful as it was to us, I may as well confess that it would excite only ridicule today, for it was a mere six horsepower voiturette, capable of twenty-five miles an hour on the level roads, but rather weak and puffy when it came to climbing hills.

We enthusiastically hit the road, passing trees and fields and houses, tasting the sweet delights of speed, all the more sweet because those indescribable delights are new to us. We are beginners, receiving our baptism of velocity; glorying in our initiation into the Order of the Knights of Speed. I am just preparing to put on that badge of brotherhood, a ferocious big pair of goggles, when suddenly a new phase of our initiation bursts upon us, bang! pss-s-ss! Oh, the horror of that sound, the hiss of that elastic serpent coiled around the right rear wheel, that flabby rubber viper that will not hold its breath long enough for us to cover half a kilometer!

But happily the telephone is everywhere in Denmark. We call up the only auto shop in town, and with a promptitude that would put to shame a fire engine or an ambulance, an emergency motor comes rushing to our rescue, bringing a new tire out from town, and before we can adjust it a second relief expedition is signaled by a cloud of dust, and soon our wrecking party is working under the orders of the proprietor of the shop, who has come all the way from town merely, as he says, "to make sure that the American gentlemen have a good day." Thanks to his good aid and that of his willing men, things are soon put to rights and we do have a good day, one of the best days I can remember, unless it be the day that followed, and the day that followed that.

SWEDEN

Glance at a map of Sweden and you will see that there is as much blue water there upon the map as there is land, for Sweden, like its neighboring country, Finland, is internally a vast fresh-water archipelago, high above sea level.

Our watery journey begins at Trollhättan where we board the canal steamer, which has been steaming along between the fields from Gothenburg to overtake us at the entrance to the locks below the town. It is always interesting to watch a steamboat go up hill, but these canal boats are such practiced stair climbers that these low hills appear to offer no obstacles to their upward course. Into the lower lock the thick-set, rotund little ship thrusts her short body; then as the lower gates are closed, sluices above are opened and the water of the second basin gushes into the first, raising the level of its waters and with it the ship, until the water in both locks stands at the same level. Then the next pair of gates is opened and the boat advances into the second lock which, closed in turn, receives part of the water from the next higher lock, through which the ascending boat will pass in its onward and upward course, that brings it ultimately to the level of the lake-like channel at the top of the long stairway up which it has come steadily and silently, rising no less than one hundred and forty-five feet from the level of the sea to that of an inland lake.

An old proverb assures us that when God divided the waters from the land He forgot all about Sweden, and this accounts for the inextricable tangle of lakes and landscapes, rivers and ridges, for the watery lanes leading across green meadows, and for the mirrory paths that wind through the woods, bringing sea-going ships even into the hillside groves, making the snorting of the marine donkey-engine as familiar to the farmer as the braying of his farmyard ass.

To travel overland by water across Sweden reminds me of those impossible dreams which come to every one of us—dreams in which we are accomplishing all sorts of curious things without the slightest sense of incongruity. We are navigating country roads in ocean steamers, plucking flowers from the waves of shrubbery that break against the sides of our ship, or promenading on a moving deck in the shade of forest trees. Certain phases of this waking dream bear the stamp of naturalness, for now and then we sweep out from the forest-bordered channels upon the bosom of lovely lakes, some of which are large enough for us to lose sight of the land in crossing them. How any traveler can be content to go by rail is quite inconceivable.

1903 ARIZONA (Hopi Land)

The fascination of the desert, the charm of the flat places of the earth, cannot be explained. It must be felt. If you would know one of the most wholesome joys of life, go buy a saddle and a bridle, a bronco and a blanket, and forgetting all the petty things of life ride away into this Sahara of our glorious Southwest, and

there find the true meaning of such words as space—exhilaration—freedom!

Volz, the Indian trader, has volunteered to be our guide, and has contracted to provide vehicles and horses to transport us to the Hopi Reservation about seventy miles away; to feed us on the best canned goods that ever come to Arizona; to see that we do not lack water more than twelve hours at a stretch; to show us the Snake Dance, and bring us safely back to the railway, all within the incredibly short space of eleven days.

Our guide has promised much, but the one thing that he failed to mention we find the most inspiring thing of all: the sense of freedom, the exhilaration of this boundless region. It has been said that it is impossible to despair on horseback. This is more than ever true in Arizona, where the air, the light, the clear, sharp distances, and the level, limitless desert form an environment that uplifts the senses and makes for perfect happiness.

At noon we halt for luncheon; but luncheon is too elegant a term, even lunch smacks too much of civilization; the proper word in Arizona for lunch is "grub." Almost everything one eats comes in a tin can or tin box: beans, milk, meat, sardines, preserves and jams—all are imported in hermetically sealed tins. Thus canned goods form a most important item in the commerce of the territory, where they are known by the comprehensive name "airtights." We breakfast, dine, and sup on airtights, and before every meal all hands are set to work with old knives and scissors, for the rare can-opener is usually missing; and by the time that the airtights have ceased to deserve the title, the workers have in the effort of opening them already developed appetites ravenous to such a degree that no time is wasted in vain longings for fresh fare. A heap of empty tins marks every halting place of every caravan, while near the site of every camp are left mountains of gaping cans.

As the Professor from Berlin remarked one day after lunch, in his staid, scientific tone, "It is my conviction that in a future age the geologists will be confronted by a novel problem, for Arizona will be found covered with a stratum of tin as extensive as the borders of the territory."

Hopi land is unique; it is a changeless corner in our land of perpetual change. The Hopis are a pueblo people, differing from other tribes of the Southwest in language, customs, and religion. They dwell in seven villages, each set like an acropolis upon a barren rock high above the barren, boundless sands of the Arizona desert.

How long they have lived there in the sunshine, no man knows. The Spaniards found them there in 1541, living and praying and performing their religious ceremonies, just as they had lived and prayed and worshiped for uncounted centuries.

These strange white men clad in armor came from the distant south. They were Spanish conquistadors, sent by Coronado to seek the Seven Cities of Cibola, thought to be rich in treasure. They found these pueblo towns upon the mesas. They tried to enter; Hopi priests protested and with sacred meal drew a line across the path. The Spaniards then bombarded with blunderbuss and bowgun, killing several Hopis. Next day the frightened mesa folk brought down gifts, welcomed the masterful strangers, and consented to build a church. The conquerors passed on, leaving a few priests to rule the Hopi villages. The people did not object to Christianity until the priests declared that all the gods of the Hopi were evil gods. This blasphemy roused the peaceful people, and they threw the "long gowns," as they called the friars, over the edge of the

◀ Doubtless the Hopi girls looked down upon the Spaniards with the same air of timid daring they exhibit today as we approach the village. If we are to credit the Spanish chroniclers, the Hopi maiden then wore her hair in the same fantastic form, and clad herself in the quaint, picturesque garments of which those of today are perfect counterparts.

The most striking feature in the make-up of the ▶ Hopi girl is her coiffure, unique among the world's hairdressing schemes. The younger girls and also many of the men wear their hair cut in the fashion of the medieval Florentines—a heavy bang on the brow, and a curtain of black tresses covering the ears and neck. The jewelry worn by the Hopi folk is marvelous: silver beads and pendants purchased from the Navajos, strings of shells with bits of common turquoise interspersed, earrings of silver inlaid with turquoise, and silver rings and bracelets chiseled with strange Navajo designs. But all the brilliant trappings of the Hopi debutante cannot distract our attention from her crowning glory. We never cease to marvel at the abundance and the jet-black spendor of her hair.

mesa, destroyed the church, and moved their villages to securer heights upon the mesa tops.

After a two-day ride and a night's rest in our desert camp, we press on to Hopi land. We gallop on for miles across the desert, a barren, yellow, world-wide avenue from which the distant mesas rise like heaps of giant pavingstones. Here and there a leafy cottonwood affords a grateful shelter from the fierce rays of an August sun. A few drought-defying plants appear,

peeping timidly from the sands, but we know that dormant seeds are everywhere, needing but the moist kiss of the infrequent storm to wake them into life.

Meanwhile our guide rides on ahead. Presently he draws rein, and pointing to the summit of the mesa exclaims, "There, Walpi." Yet, where is the town of Walpi? We know it stands upon this sandstone mesa—but we are not yet able to distinguish it. The steep slope terminates in what appears to be a mass of titanic blocks of stone resembling a natural citadel.

Portrait of a Hopi man.

There they are free to wander all over town, leaving us to the empty streets and deserted plazas.

A pueblo village is practically one structure. The streets and alleyways are roofed with rooms; the entrance to one house is often found upon the roof of the dwelling of a neighbor. There are ladders and stone stairways everywhere, and these are used more generally than the streets and squares below. We visited the three villages on this mesa, Mishongnovi, a higher village called Shipaulovi, "The Place of the Peaches," and Shungopavi.

The people of each village are divided into many clans, and each clan is regarded as a family. Its members may not intermarry; they must wed the sons and

Perhaps the town lies on the other side. But no, the guide insists that we are very near; and when a moment later our horses stumble round another angle of the trail, the cyclopean citadel resolves itself into a Hopi village. What seemed gigantic cubes of stone are small pueblo dwellings. Walpi, which from below was indistinguishable, reveals itself as a place of human habitation only to those who scale the cliffs.

Only the old men are found at home today; the active male population is in the distant fields guarding the corn, the melons, and the beans, leaving the village in possession of the aged, the women, and the children. At our first approach the children fled like a lot of prairie-dogs, popping into the underground rooms, or kivas, dashing through low doorways into cube-like dwellings, or running up the ladders to the housetops.

Portrait of a Hopi elder.

110

Portrait of a Hopi elder.

dressmaking—the husband always weaving the wedding garment for the bride—but weaving it so well that it will last the wife a lifetime, and then possibly serve a daughter until marriage. The shawls of brilliant calico, however, are purchased from the trader.

Kopele, chief priest of the Snake Fraternity.

daughters of some other clan. There are seven villages in all. The natives number about twenty-five hundred, of whom eight hundred live in Oraibi, which is the largest of the villages.

Evidently the population is increasing, for as soon as we produce big bags of colored candies and begin a distribution, young Hopi hopefuls begin to spring up like desert weeds under the influence of a sudden deluge. A few minutes of this bombardment of bonbons, and all timidity is banished. We are accepted as "good people," and the entire village is ours to explore.

We notice the dress of the girls and old women: a heavy blanket-like robe, the black body separated from the blue border by stripes of brilliant green. Around the waist is worn a woven sash. All these things are of domestic manufacture; in fact, the men do all the

◀ The babies of Hopi land lead a happy life. Water is so precious here that none is wasted in those unnecessary and annoying scrubbings. The tub has no terror for the urchins of these towns. They bathe only in the clear dry air, wash their faces in sunshine, comb their hair with the sharp wind from the desert, and are as healthy as the children of the poor in any land. They are wonderfully self-reliant. The town is an intricate apartment-house with steep stairways and tall crude ladders as the only means of communications between floor and floor. But babies that can barely creep on level ground develop at a very early age a daring familiarity with the ups and downs of life.

CALIFORNIA (Yosemite)

Everyone who visits Yosemite goes out on the celebrated overhanging rock, that natural balcony that plunges down a sheer three thousand feet. There is probably no dizzier viewpoint accessible to ordinary tourists anywhere in this wide world, no view point at the same time so perilous and yet so little feared. Foolhardy folk have cut all kinds of capers on that ledge of loosened rock, for it *is* loose, it can be made to teeter just a little. For instance, the exploit of the auto run out to the verge—but how did the auto get there in the first place? Makes you wonder!

There must be a reason for and a design in all this perfect harmony of beauty, grandeur and impressiveness. A wonder scene like this cannot be simply the result of geologic accident or chance.

We thirst to know how this has come to be the wonderfully lovely sight it is, why God should give to man a

gift like this. Surely man has not merited so beautiful a gift, but we accept it gratefully, and resolve in the presence of a scene like this to cultivate appreciation of the beautiful in Nature and in Art.

▲ This tiny village in Yosemite is a patriotic little corner of our country as we discover on the morning of the Glorious Fourth of July. Equestrian companies come dashing in from distant camps, while other campers come in decorated wagons—for it has been an-

nounced that the Motion Picture man is to be on hand and the entire population has come in its well-varied array to have its Motion Picture taken.

Never before, we are assured, has there been such a spectacular demonstration—in fact, this is the first Fourth of July parade ever organized in the Yosemite. The "Mayor," not satisfied with the slow pace of the procession, clamors for more animation, and organizing a squadron of Campers Cavalry, sends them thundering past us in lively western fashion.

ALASKA (The Klondike)

The whole history of humanity's quest for gold has been epitomized within the last six years by the sensational series of events that followed the finding of gold in 1896 in the far northwest corner of our continent.

Within six years a vast, almost unknown and unpeopled region has become one of the most discussed, most variously peopled, and most rapidly progressive regions in the world.

115

Shooting a picture on the Yukon River.

Alaska and the Klondike as they are today are among the most amazing facts of our new century; yesterday a wilderness with heroes fighting epic battles with the elements; today a land of towns and cities with happy homes and thriving business enterprises. Where in the world is there a region which within two thousand days has been rushed from lonely desolation into the dignity of an established commonwealth.

From White Horse down to Dawson I had for highway the great rapid-flowing river and for conveyance the comfortable Yukon steamers that ply all summer up and down the stream. Our voyage was made in two days and two short nights. We suffered some delay when we went to the assistance of another steamer in distress, taking her passengers and possessions on board. The other steamer was carrying miners to the scene of a strike, and her pilot dropped asleep and struck a rocky cliff head, and the steamer refused to budge. Her hull was damaged and her decks strewn with bits of rock she had gutted from the cliff. The miners, in the excitement, true to the spirit of the prospector, picked up and pocketed these quartz samples.

Though Dawson was a busy place I found a large leisure class. Its members sit or stand there all day idle, nor do they seek that any man should hire them. They

117

Dawson City street scene.

Dawson City street scene.

Home Sweet Home.

Telephone operators sit on wooden barrels.

bestir themselves only when the sun begins to bleach the sidewalk, transferring themselves with an air of injured dignity to a shady stretch of sidewalk just around the corner.

1904 SWITZERLAND

The traveler goes to Switzerland chiefly to look at mountains; the Swiss Alps are as effectively displayed as the treasures in a well-arranged museum. But the mountains are not the only things in Switzerland. There are the towns and cities and the people, those admirable Swiss people, who have made their land in many respects the model country of the world.

Although Switzerland may be the playground of Europe, it is not the playground of the Swiss. It is their workshop, where they toil at many industries, and practice many useful arts of which the outside world knows little. We know only that they make music-boxes, cheese, and watches; and that they are the best hotel-keepers in the world. But to say that they are a nation of hotel-keepers is to make poor return for all the comforts and courtesies we owe to those who have been our hosts in Switzerland. The traveler has cause in many lands to thank the Swiss, who have made the management of hotels an art, and sent forth missionaries to practice and to teach that art in the lands of the outer barbarians.

No traveler feels that he has quite reached the heart of Switzerland until he finds himself at Zermatt. It is

The Matterhorn seen from Zermatt.

preeminently the headquarters of the alpinist. The town is always full of climbers—the ice-axe is the ordinary walking stick, and everybody wears spiked shoes and green hats adorned with edelweiss, a coil of rope and a rucksack. The magnet that draws most people to Zermatt, I need not name. I need not even point it out. It is there, you cannot miss it—it is everywhere, the most self-assertive mountain in the world, the most astonishing in outline, the most savage in form, the coldest, cruelest-looking peak that Nature ever fashioned in her favorite rock-garden of the Alps.

Alpine climbers are not made; like fools they must be ▲ born with a contempt for those perils that the wise man in his wisdom would not seek.

The Jungfrau was first climbed about a hundred years ago. It is now climbed every year, and every year the Jungfrau claims her victims. The very day I came, two men died there amid the snows. They were skilled climbers, but they were not able to cope with storm and chance—those evil geniuses of every mountaineer. [See colorplate on page 135]

123

The Fête des Vignerons is the vintners' thanksgiving celebration. During the Fête, Vevey's streets are alive with the gods and goddesses, the fauns and nymphs, satyrs and bacchantes of mythology. A stranger dropping into town, not knowing that a festival was on, would imagine himself enjoying a delightful classic nightmare.

But what we see in the streets is nothing compared with the great spectacle presented in the arena of the ▶ huge amphitheater in the presence of audiences of thirteen thousand persons. More than eighteen hundred characters appear in the colossal production. The orchestra is made up of three symphony orchestras and two military bands. The music is good music; it has the dignity and genuineness of the native folk song, with a beauty and poetic grace that one would not expect to find in a mere peasant festival.

A Japanese regiment.

This destructive war developed out of colonial rivalries between Russia and Japan. Russia had penetrated Korea and Manchuria (spheres of influence claimed by Japan) and had hardened the intrusion by refusing to negotiate.

Japan laid siege on Port Arthur, bottling up the Russian battleships in the harbor. By 1905, the Japanese had captured the port, scattered the Russians at Mukden, and obliterated the Russian fleet at Tsushima. President Theodore Roosevelt mediated a truce between the warring nations. The conflict proved such a debacle for Russia that the demoralized armed forces mutinied, leading to the abortive Revolution of 1905.

Japanese activity against Port Arthur was practically continuous for ten months and twenty days. The siege proper, after the taking of the outer series of defences, lasted four months and nineteen days.

There were seven grand assaults. The failure of the first with its terrible loss of life, a list of killed and wounded twenty-five thousand long, taught General Nogi that he could not charge into Port Arthur's forts. He would have to dig his way in, his men would have to lay aside their rifles and take up the weapons that ultimately won the citadel, the pick, the spade, and the straw basket in which each night the fresh earth was carried the whole length of the trench and dumped out at the rear, for it would never do to heap it up along the rim and have the Russian gunners discover the precise whereabouts of the invisible attacking forces.

His Excellency General Count Maresuke Nogi: conqueror of the strongest fortress ever reared by man, successful director of the most marvelous military operations in the history of war, the executive genius of

The Russian Imperial Army on horseback.

Count Maresuke Nogi.

A Russian funeral service on the battlefield.

St. Basil the Blessed, The Kremlin, Moscow, 1901.

View of the Kremlin across the Moskva River.

Marble bridge in the Forbidden City, Peking, 1901.

Interior at the Imperial Palace, Forbidden City, Peking, 1901.

Swiss bar maids, 1904.

Mountain climbers on the Jungfrau, Switzerland, 1904.

The Russian artillery.

A mortar bursting, Russo-Japanese War, 1905.

Osaka Baby spitting a shell into the air.

The Russian fleet sinking.

All of the ships have been riddled, first, horizontally by shells from Togo's fleet, then vertically, raked up and down, from bridge to bunker, from deck to keel, by the shells from the big guns concealed three miles away behind the hills, unseen but not inaudible, and feared, as man always fears that which he cannot see and against which there is absolutely no defense.

the siege who carried into effect with masterly ability the seemingly impossible designs framed by another genius, General Kodama.

Brains played the most important part at Port Arthur; the Russians proved the utter uselessness of sacrifice and courage when not directed by a master mind. Japan was happy in possessing master minds; men of amazing intellect were those who planned the moves made on that fateful chessboard that lay beneath Port Arthur's deep-set forts and firmly mounted guns.

Tactical preparations were among the most amazing feats of the incredible epic—the placing of the Japanese big guns. These canon, the coast defense guns of Japan, had to be brought by sea to Dalny, already taken by the Japanese. Thence they were brought by rail inland, but only to a point on the edge of the danger zone, several miles distant from the sites that they must occupy in order to do their work as it must be done, effectively, accurately, fatally.

These guns, intended only for permanent emplacements in the modern coast defenses of Japan, weighed seventeen tons each; their mouths were eleven inches wide; the shells that they spit forth weighed five hundred pounds each, as much as three strong men. The roads, or rather the open country over which these great guns had to be hauled was soft and

rough, and there was not a square rod of well-placed rocky ground to serve as natural foundation. The thing appeared impossible, yet it was done; perfectly sound foundations made of the best cement were put in at the right spot by the engineers of the Mikado, ofttimes working under Russian fire.

These ready, word was given and eight hundred men sprang to their ropes and, tugging in the grandest tug-of-war that soldiers ever pulled, those men brought the great guns of Osaka, called "The Osaka Babies," to their playground, muffling the squealing of the axles, lightening the toil with that peculiar rhythm that makes concerted labor easy.

Thus were the big Osaka Babies, so obstinate in their immoveability, wheedled out of their railway carriages and coaxed across country to play their awful game, each in the charge of a thousand nurses, their thousand faces lighted by a thousand willing smiles; smiles that mocked at this Herculean labor and defied whizzing, whirring Russian shells that now and then arched overhead.

That is how the big guns were brought into position, and installed upon their deep cement emplacements as firmly as if planted there permanently. All this work done, we must remember within range of Russian forts. Was ever engineering work done and well done under conditions more seemingly prohibitive? Nor was it done without cost. Fighting has been going on all this time; bullets and shell fragments have been finding that which they were sent to seek, dead men and wounded have been carried to the rear by Chinese coolies; some days by dozens, other days by hundreds. Then the days of those impossible assaults by the thousands; and finally the days when the dead could not be given burial, when even the wounded could not be reached on the contested slopes, so fierce and so deadly the insistent rain of lead.

Cossacks.

1906 NAPLES (The Eruption of Vesuvius)

There is no mountain in the world that has so terrible a reputation as Vesuvius. The Alps, the Andes, the Rockies, the Himalayas are from four to seven times as high, but they are all dead mountains—Vesuvius is alive. Vesuvius rises almost in the suburb of the most populous city in all Italy.

Chance made us eye-witnesses of the last Vesuvian eruption, which began on April 8, 1906. We entered the harbor of Naples on the very eve of the most terrific outburst that had occurred in modern times. It was too late for us to land, and we retired to our cabins, utterly unconscious of the impending tragedy— saying as we bade one another good night, "How well Vesuvius looks tonight. We must go up tomorrow to the crater by Cook's railway." We did not know that while we slept that night in harbor, Cook's railway would be swallowed by the crater, and that part of the cone itself would cave in and be blown out again in atoms, rising in a dusty cloud to a height of several thousand feet before it settled down on the surrounding region. But we found some of that pulverized cone scattered all over town, like dirty, grayish talcum powder, as we drove next morning from the landing place to our hotel.

We found the hotel crowded with visitors. That Sunday morning, April 8th, we secured the only vacant room; by Wednesday, April 11th, my companions and myself and one other guest had the hotel all to ourselves. The others had all fled as fast as they could get away. By Wednesday the entire railway system of the south was at a standstill, the lines blocked or buried by the cinder-storms. The streets of Naples were alive with the pitiful processions of the terror-stricken

populace—women with streaming hair loaded with grayish ashes, and small boys with the dirt of Naples powdered over with that same gray volcanic powder, paraded through every street, carrying crucifixes, candles, and the image of a saint or a Madonna.

It was not until Monday morning, twenty-four hours after we had landed, that Vesuvius was seen at all from Naples. All day Sunday a grimy haze hid everything; but Monday morning the wind changed, and the smoke that had turned all the world to a gray nothingness retired—took shape in the distance, and finally resolved itself into that terrible Vesuvian pigna, that awful, dreaded shape described by Pliny, eighteen hundred years ago, as being like a huge umbrella pine—a tree with a trunk of rising smoke and spreading branches all of curling smoke, a tree six thousand feet in height and rooted in a burning crater that is itself four thousand feet above the sea. Never has humanity seemed more absurdly unimportant and Nature more brutally and grandly omnipotent, than during the hours when we stand and watch that awesome, tremendous "pine-tree," out of its vague shapelessness taking shape before our eyes.

It must be understood that on the fatal night of the 7th and the morning of the 8th of April conditions were such that no pictures could be taken. We could not even see what was then going on. The first catastrophe of which we had definite confirmation was the overwhelming of the village of Boscotrecase, near Pompeii, by a stream of lava. This happened between two and four o'clock, in the darkness that preceded dawn. We reached the place twelve hours later. We found a sea of black stuff, like huge chunks of charcoal, lying ten to twenty feet deep over an area of many acres, with here and there a housetop rising from the mass.

Destruction in quite a different form was meantime

descending on the district that lies behind the mountain, on the landward side of Vesuvius. But that district is now inaccessible. Night has come on and we are fifteen miles from Naples, to which we must return for food, rest, and above all, plates and films, for we must use on every subject a dozen plates in order to be sure of getting one good picture under these conditions, the like of which we never met before.

Never shall I forget our return drive to Naples. At first fatigue was all that bothered us; then night came suddenly, and with it a strange smothering sensation, noticeable chiefly in the eyes, as if our eyes were being smothered; then they began to itch; then we began to rub them; then we kept them closed until the driver said, "Please take the reins a moment while I clean my

eyes—I cannot see." No more could we, unless we cleaned our smarting eyes every two minutes. By this time the air was thick with flying ashes—powdery and bitter as pulverized quinine. It was like driving through a blackish blizzard of heavy, clinging, penetrating, dirty, dried-up snow. The stuff got in our noses, and in our mouths, and ears; every jolt shook it in showers from our hats and shoulders, and it took the three of us to steer the blinded horse along the now almost deserted street that curves for fifteen miles around the bay toward distant Naples. We could see nothing save a dim gas-lamp here and there—quickly extinguished, so far as concerned us, by a sudden swirling of the ashy clouds. We knew that behind and above all this Vesuvius was waking to new activity; and worse, we knew that the wind was now toward Naples, and that there would be no end to our petty tortures even there. Then we began to wonder if something worse might not be coming.

We arrived safely, and the next day, rested and resupplied, we set out for the towns that lay behind the mountain, on the side fartherest from the sea. These towns had been almost completely overwhelmed, not by lava, for none had flowed down on that side; not by ashes, for no fine stuff had fallen there; but by cinders—big gritty cinders. The nearer we get to the unhappy towns, the deeper the flood of cinders. We meet hundreds of refugees trudging along, carrying bundles on their heads and babies in their arms, not knowing where to go, having no money and no homes, thinking of nothing save their dull desire to get beyond the reach of that awful rain of cinders which has already crushed their houses, killed their neighbors, and is now pursuing them as if bent on destroying every inhabitant of this once happy region known as the Campagna Felice, or the Happy Country. A terrible obscurity fills the sky and follows them like a black wall of solid stuff, reaching from the pale earth up to a heaven that is black and ominous: yet behind us the sky is clear and blue and beautiful.

Blacker and blacker grows the air, until it is as black as night with an almost opaque blackness—a blackness that we can positively feel. It is a rain of ashes, not of cinders; but there are already cinders underfoot, and we crunch our slow way over miles of cindery roads to San Giuseppe, a town that had been gutted by a cyclone of hot cinders. Some people fled, some took refuge in the church. They thought the house of God would stand even if all else failed. They put too much trust in their poor old church; roof, cinders, ceiling, all crashed down upon that congregation; and out of the

two hundred who were praying there, less than sixty lived to tell how the rest perished.

Now the treacherous, terrible volcano sleeps its old half-troubled slumber—to sleep a harmless sleep perhaps for centuries—perhaps, who knows, to wake again in awful and destructive majesty before another day has passed.

ATHENS (The Second Olympiad)

The finish of the 800-meter run. Paul Pilgrim is the winner, J.D. Lightbody a close second. Both are Americans.

———————

Happy indeed should be the lives of all these victors if ▶ the poet's words be true, for Pindar, who wrote many odes honoring those who bore off the highest prizes in olden games, informs us that "He who overcometh hath because of the Games a sweet tranquillity throughout his life forevermore."

EGYPT

To go to Egypt is to go back to the beginning of human history. Beyond Egypt lies primeval mystery. The earliest pyramid marks the frontier between the unknown and the known, and in the wilderness of centuries that rolls between that pyramid and the oldest works of man in other lands, the only conspicuous milestones are the other pyramids, and the other Egyptian monuments that rise along the Nile. For more than a score of centuries the world was Egypt, and Egypt was the world.

Cairo becomes, every winter, the Mecca of those cosmopolitan pilgrims of pleasure whose other sacred places are the Riviera, Palm Beach, Paris, London and New York. We arrive by rail and drive directly to Shepheard's, the original big caravansary for Christians in this Moslem city. There are now many other big hotels, some bigger, even more luxurious, but Shepheard's remains the heart and center of the foreign life of Cairo. The terrace of this hotel is one of the famous meeting-places for world-wanderers, a half-way halting place in their race around the world. Not to know Shepheard's Terrace is a social crime. The traveler who has not trod the tile pavement of this terrace is little better than a stay-at-home, and the woman of fashion who has not sipped tea at the tables on the terrace dares not look five o'clock in the face.

Man made, but man cannot destroy, the Pyramids. The Pyramids are destined to perish only with the world. "All things fear Time, but Time fears the Pyramids."

Never to be forgotten is the moment when I first beheld the outlines of those solid shapes, gigantic and triangular, that stand for all the glory and the dignity of the Egypt of the past. I murmur, "The Pyramids!" That is all that should be said: "The Pyramids!" All history is breathed in that one word, the story of our race from today back to the dim beginning. Who looks upon the Pyramids for the first time keeps silence; they represent terrestrial Eternity, they almost paralyze imagination, because they alone of all the works of man bid fair to conquer Time. [See also colorplate on page 209]

▲ Who does not know this face and form, who need be told the name of the huge thing, speechless but eloquent. Today, battered and broken by the attacks of Time and Man, this personification of mystery is flat-faced and featureless, its head the stony semblance of a human skull; but I feel sure that once this mutilated mask was beautiful.

────────────

There are three usual ways of going up the Nile—by rail, by dahabiyeh, or by excursion steamer. To go up by rail is to miss absolutely the charm of the trip, to sail up in a dahabiyeh is very costly both in money and time, and therefore most people go by one of the tourist steamers that make the regular cruise up to the second cataract and back to Cairo in twenty-one days. We make our Nile cruise in the "Nemo," a little steam yacht. The "Nemo" is manned by seventeen men. There is the captain, who is also chief steward, a German; waiters, Nubians; the chef and his assistant, Arabs; the engineer, a villain; the assistant engineer and stoker, so soiled that nationality did not show

Grandma Burton travels in style.

through the grime; four sailors, Nubian and native; a chief pilot, more like a monkey than a man; three other pilots picked up at various ports, and last, but never least, the dragoman, Gattas George, a Coptic Christian and as kindly a soul as I've ever encountered.

Some say the Nile voyage is monotonous, but one who loves color and pictures will never find it so. We are kept on the continual qui vive for the color effects which come and go with every passing hour and for fine compositions formed and framed in every passing mile.

To our amazement we find many a mile of the river walled in on one side or the other by the high cliffs of rocky hills that rise upon the Libyan or the Arabian shores. The Nile boasts palisades surpassing those of the Hudson, and at times suggesting in form and coloring even the walls of the Grand Canyon of the Colorado. There is many a surprise in Egypt for the traveler who comes with notions fixed or preconceived. So, shattering preconceptions every day and every mile, we make our way with the aid of time and the tired engines of the "Nemo" against the current of the waters, but with the currents of the air, for the

The full face of a Nile felucca is always distingué and ▶ beautiful, but the profile is distinctly disappointing. Thus all depends on the point of view; head-on, the boats are fairy craft, graceful as gorgeous insects on the wing; on the quarter they have already lost their magical perfection of proportion, and when at last we overtake one and view it as it glides along abeam, the splendid argosy has become an ordinary scow, and the glorious, full-winged butterfly has grown scrawny and as awkward as a humble sand-fly.

prevailing winds are from the south. It is a curious fact that it is easy to sail up the Nile, but very difficult to sail down the river, for the winds are stronger than the current.

▼ At the port of Suez we enter the Canal and find ourselves in the narrow ditch, the completion of which in 1869 shifted the commercial currents of the modern world. The Suez Canal, conceived by the great Frenchman Ferdinand de Lesseps and paid for chiefly with French gold, is now practically a possession of Great Britain. Its absolute neutrality in time of war is guaranteed by treaties. Its actual operation is still in the hands of the French—but its enormous earnings go to England in the form of dividends. The cutting of this trough a hundred miles, from the Red Sea to the Mediterranean, cost eighty million dollars and ten years time—but it was child's play as compared with the cutting of the Canal of Panama. No mountains here—no elevations—just a level stretch of desert sand—easy to shift—and two salty bitter basins dug by obliging Nature half way across the isthmus make Man's task the easier. Ships traverse the Canal in sixteen hours from Suez to Port Said, where we drop anchor before the palatial administration building of the Canal Company.

Harbor scene in Port Said.

A TYPHOON IN HONG KONG

These pictures were taken during the terrible typhoon of September 18, 1906, which came without the usual warning. As a rule our observatory in Manila warns Hong Kong in time for the shipping to prepare for the big blow. The liners get up steam and get out extra lines and anchors; the little junks and native craft seek refuge in the special inner typhoon harbor.

But this storm came the landward direction, unannounced. In two hours time the storm took an enor-mous number of lives, no one will ever know the exact number.

By 9:30 A.M. the blackness of despair had fallen on the souls of all the living who clung to craft remaining afloat. The wind is driving a heavy wall of rain across the harbor at the rate of 150 miles an hour. So dense is the downpour that it hides many of the sinking ships. Junks are hammering themselves to pieces here on the stone wharf. Ten minutes later, one junk has succeeded in its suicidal effort and the waves are washing over the wharf. Meantime a big river steamer had battered holes in herself and gone down. Ocean liners in the harbor dragged their anchors and collided or else rammed themselves into wrecks along the Kowloon shore.

By 10:00 the typhoon had eaten about all there was in sight. A typhoon usually blows for ten to eleven hours. This one did its work in less than two. By noon the sun was shining, and by 2:00 P.M. the stillness of death had fallen upon the waters. There are remnants of the pier through which a launch had battered her way, followed by a flotilla of junks on their dash toward the stone wharf where they were utterly annihilated.

Fifty percent of the native shipping in these waters was completely wiped out and an estimate of eight to ten thousand men, women, and children did not resume, that afternoon, their fight for existence amid the crowded competition of this, the greatest sea port in the world.

1907 PARIS

To thoroughly enjoy the real Paris, the stranger, too, should learn the Parisian art of flânerie. Flâner is the verb that stands for "loaf," but it is a more graceful word than "loaf," and the art itself, or rather the passive state of being a flâneur, is far removed from the vulgarity of loafing as practiced in other less artistic countries. The art of flânerie is a fine art with the French, and in the parks of Paris we may observe the real Parisians, enjoying life in their own sensible and quiet way. Parisians utterly unlike those of the garish boulevards. [See colorplate on page 211]

The history of Nôtre Dame and its site is the history of Paris. Here stood an altar to Jupiter in the old pagan days when Paris was a Roman stronghold. Here also rose a little Christian church in the fourth century; in the great church that we see today many a King of France was crowned. Here Bonaparte crowned himself Emperor of the French and placed a crown upon the head of Josephine. Here Napoleon III was married to the beautiful Eugénie. Here the ruffians of the Commune tried to duplicate their destructive successes at the Tuileries and the Hôtel de Ville; for having destroyed the palace that was the symbol of Imperial authority, and the City Hall which was the symbol of law and order, they attempted to put an end to Nôtre Dame, the symbol of religion. But Nôtre Dame was not of perishable stuff. The church that had combatted the eternal fires for so many centuries was not to fall a prey to those short-lived anarchistic flames.

156

VIENNA

This superb edifice [see colorplate on page 210] on the Ringstrasse is the Grand Opera House, which yields in splendor only to its Paris rival. In fact, if one has never seen the latter, the Austrian temple of music will seem unsurpassed in the sumptuous decorations of its staircase, portico, and foyer; while the auditorium, which has a seating capacity for two thousand five hundred, is decorated far more pleasantly and with less ostentatious gilding than that of Paris.

Late-comers to a performance in this opera house are not allowed to disturb the audience already assembled. No one is permitted to take his seat during the overture; and in Wagner's operas, where there is no intermission between the overture and the first act, those who come late are not allowed to go to their seats until the curtain falls.

It is, after all, well to insist on punctuality, and such heroic measures are, no doubt, necessary to enforce it. There is no good reason why several thousand spectators should have their attention diverted from an opera, which they have paid a high price to hear, by the arrival of persons who are careless or thoughtless enough to come late. It is needless to add that, at the Vienna opera, no woman is allowed to annoy people by wearing a large hat.

BERLIN

Berlin cannot be called a stylish city; that is, what we are pleased to call style is rarely seen. There is no German "Gibson Girl" and no Teutonic "Fluffy Ruffles." There are no amazing creatures robed like birds of paradise such as we see in Paris, and even the lady of the trim-cut tailor-made is conspicuously absent.

Instead we see fine, wholesome types of womanhood, who waste no time on niceties of dress; they are content merely to be well clad. Their clothes are not creations, they are merely clothes; their hats are not "dreams" as in Paris, not "nightmares" as ofttimes in New York—they are simply hats. The Marcel wave will never swamp Berlin.

Today there are nearly three million people living in Berlin. Of these one man stands out as the most conspicuous, pervading personality of living Germany—the Kaiser.

William the Second is everywhere, interested in all things, active in all things, himself in all things. He has an insatiable appetite for information: as a giver of advice he is indefatigable. We see him in photographs or in person questioning his admirals on the bridges of his warships, directing his staff officers at military maneuvers or reviewing troops on the Tempelhoferfeld. We see him as an equestrian in the Tiergarten, as a pedestrian in Unter-den-Linden or as the helmeted

▲ The world now looks almost with awe upon the German laborer—the Teutonic builder, strong, patient, painstaking, content with little pay. The toiler of new Germany, as typified by the splendid specimen of manhood in our illustration, looks a reincarnation of some northern god.

war-lord in the imperial car, motoring like a hurricane from Mars across the Potsdamer Platz. Berlin without the Kaiser would seem to lack one-half of its three million population.

The Kaiser holds in his grasp the mightiest instrument of war ever forged by any nation, the biggest and most perfect fighting machine the world has ever seen—the German army—the most potent guarantee of peace, the most portentous agent of destruction in the modern world. Germany stands today secure in her preparedness.

From the position of a poverty-stricken and war-ravaged agricultural nation, Germany has advanced to that of a rich, peace-preserving industrial nation whose little label "Made in Germany" has made its triumphant way around the world, upsetting the economic equilibrium of many a manufacturing community. All this amazing progress along the paths of peace has been made to the sound of military music, but at the same time the rattle of the loom has been heard above the clank of the saber, the racket of the steel riveters above the roar of rifle practice, and the mental processes of the German master minds in chemistry and in all the scientific industries have done more for Germany than all the maneuvers of her army or the strategic cruises of her fleets.

Has Germany succeeded because of her preparedness for war, or has she succeeded in spite of it? Her military preeminence and her increasing naval prominence cost her people dear, for in addition to the enormous expenditures made by the government for the equipment and maintenance of her great army and navy there must be added the enormous total made up of the modest sums provided by devoted families for the support of the young men during their period of service in the ranks or on the seas. Thus the German

The Kaiser.

Prussian army barracks.

people support their soldiers and their sailors, not only indirectly through taxation, but directly by sending, from time to time, the little sums that make life possible for a self-respecting wearer of the Kaiser's uniform.

But is all that crushing military burden necessary? This is the question asked by the "plain people," the tax-payers, as they stand in the presence of the great War Giant they have bred and reared and which they now have to feed and clothe and keep supplied with powder and with steel. Is this monstrous thing of blood and discipline—this German army—worth what it costs the people in gold, in labor, and in sacrifice? This is the question which Humanity is asking. The War Lord has his answer ready. His people may find yet another. Let us hope that the answer will not be one that will shake the foundations of civilization, that the guiding hand of him who sits upon the German throne and the sturdy common sense of those who call him Kaiser, may so wisely control this unparalleled incarnation of military power—this army of the Father-land—that it may never, like the monster made by Frankenstein, become a thing that even its creator cannot master.

———————

The Spreewald is the last non-Germanized stronghold ▶ of the Wendish folk, who cling to all their old-time ways and customs. Their cottages are quainter and more picturesque than those of their German neighbors, and their costumes are the quaintest and most picturesque that can be found in any part of Germany today.

We were so fortunate as to drop in at the out-of-door studio of the village photographer just in time to see these two particularly charming damsels posing for their pictures. With their consent and that of our professional confrère we clicked our hand-cameras sev-

eral times while he was getting ready to make a long time-exposure with his cumbrous old-style outfit. Possibly the dresses and the head-dress are a little more elaborate than would be worn every day; but the frank honest faces, the strong bare arms, and the happy dispositions pictured here are characteristic of the younger women in this district. Even the older women, the mothers of the Wendish tribe, seem to preserve the same attractive physical wholesomeness and the same kindly attitude of soul.

164

Mount Fuji.

1908 JAPAN

Japan is blessed with natural beauty in its mountains and valleys, its trees and flowers, its rivers and seas, and the thousands of religious structures were almost invariably placed amidst these fascinating scenes. The result is an indefinable artistry that pervades the entire Empire.

The Inland Sea.

The Inland Sea is one of the most fascinating bodies of water in the world. There is a strangeness about everything. Even the skyline of the mountains looks as if it had been cut by a Japanese artist, and the boats that glide so silently seem like dream ships, or phantom craft, sketched in by one of the old masters of oriental art, inspired by some magic spell. There is a sense of unreality about the whole scene, too strange, too quaint, and too beautiful to be really true.

The temples of Kyoto seem almost numberless, and ▶ yet I found at the time of this visit two new temples rising from the heart of this long-since-completed city. Incredible, indeed, but true it is, that old wise Kyoto, not content with her three thousand half-deserted temples, must needs construct two more and make them grander, finer, and more enormous than any of the boasted structures of the past.

What is more marvelous, the larger structure, the Higashi Hongwanji, rises, not with the aid of government or prince, as did the ancient shrines, but owes its being to the common people and the peasants, who, by gifts of money and material, of time and labor, have rendered possible this mighty undertaking. Clever carpenters have given their strength and skill to shape into pillars the gigantic trees that have been cut down and hauled to the city as offerings by worshipers whose homes are in far-distant forests.

Those who had nothing to give yet gave something; witness the gigantic coils of rope, indeed the strangest offering of all, and the most pathetic, for they are made of human hair. Yes, poor peasant women, destitute of all save their wealth of raven hair, sacrificed even their crowning glory, and, braiding their jet black tresses into mighty ropes, sent them to be employed in hauling timber for the construction of the temple. One of these cables is three hundred and sixty feet in length and nearly three inches in diameter.

And, now, the work accomplished, these coils of human hair remain as a memorial of the faith of unknown thousands of pious, gentle souls who have not hesitated to make sacrifice, at the call of duty, even of their good looks. And yet we have been told that Buddhism is a dying faith!

At the Temple of the Thirty-three Thousand Gods, we may see at one glance more deities than we could see in a pilgrimage of forty days. The interior suggests a grandstand at a Jubilee procession, filled with spectators from some strange oriental paradise. A glittering company of heavenly beings is assembled here as if to witness some imposing ceremony; nor do we see them all.

Behind us are massed an equal number of silent brazen figures, a host of Amazons, bristling with innumerable arms and weapons, their heads encircled by elaborate golden halos, their faces wreathed in the same supercilious oriental smile—that smile with which the gods of the East look down upon terrestrial events.

It was very early this morning before it began to rain in Kyoto. As the hours went by, the air grew so full of water that it could not hold any more, and the rain began. The grayness has gone out of the world, and the colors have come back. ▶

It rains so much of the time in Japan that people are quite used to it, and it doesn't trouble them at all. They clatter along on their high rain shoes, walking as

though they were on little stilts. Over their heads they carry big, flat umbrellas made of heavy, oiled paper on bamboo frames. These umbrellas shed water like a duck's back. When you have shaken off the big drops, they are as dry as ever.

The wrestlers of Japan are all big men. They are called Sumo, or Sumo-tori, and while they form a class apart, they are full-blooded Japanese, phenomenal sons of ordinary people. Because a career in the ring offers such rich rewards, parents of burly offspring usually dedicate their big boy babies to this sport and give them over at a tender age to be trained in this ancient and profitable art.

The great wrestling matches are to the Sumo-fanatics what the big league games are to baseball fans of America.

I have witnessed several of these colossal tournaments in Tokyo, where the ring is under a roof, in a great building erected especially for the contests. But it is at a minor tournament in a small town that we may best observe the Sumo in action at close range. There are, so to speak, major leagues and minor leagues of Sumo. They are a fine body of men. They wear cues, tightly curled, like the bull-fighters of Spain, and for the formal introduction ceremony, richly embroidered aprons presented to them by admirers. The ring is formed by sixteen rice bales arranged in a circle, under a four-post canopy. The umpire wears the old-time formal Kami-shimo dress, corresponding to our frock coat for state occasions. He carries a curious fan with which he makes his signal to contestants. In former days he wore a short sword, to be prepared to commit hara-kiri in case he should disgrace himself by rendering a wrong decision! In other words, he was ready for the cry of, "Kill the umpire," and ready to

beat the public to the execution. There are forty-eight fair hands or grips. If so much as a foot is forced outside the ring, the owner of the foot is "out."

In spite of their great weight, the men are supple. Their flesh has been hardened by batting at wooden posts, until it is like tempered metal. The famous Sumo-Taiho once challenged anyone to kick him in the stomach. The challenge was accepted by an American football champion, who for the test was allowed to wear his walking boots. The wrestler braced himself, and as the kick was delivered shot his great stomach forward and sent the ball player flying as if projected by a catapult.

◄ The children of Japan are fascinating. The well-bred baby always wears a shaven pate, with here and there a tuft of hair left by maternal fantasy, either as a bit of decoration or a mark to distinguish her child from the amazingly similar baby belonging to the family next door.

The region of Noborebetsu on the island of Hokkaido ► is famous for its hot springs. This region combines the colorful beauty of a Japanese Yellowstone Park with the terror of a Japanese Vesuvius.

Most people who go to Noborebetsu go not to see the sights but to bathe for their health. The water is led down a valley, and it cascades from wooden spouts into the bathing-place. Of course it cools off a little on the way, but even so it is terribly hot. People with rheumatism or other troubles stand, or lie, under these spouts where the water will fall on their aching joints and back. The cure is almost as painful as the disease!

The summer of my Norway tour seems to me now, as I recall it, like a long, magnificent dream of the impossible, a splendid scenic nightmare filled with an endless succession of sensations as overpowering and unforgettable as the scenes that inspired them were stupendously impressive. Nature herself has set us an example of extravagance unapproached anywhere on earth. In Norway, ice, the elder brother of the liquid element, has performed miracles, of which the testimonies are the fjords, those terrible gashes in the breast of the Scandinavian peninsula—gashes that are deeper than the ocean and are cleft in mountains, the slopes of which descend from the line of perpetual snow to meet in the depths of submarine gorges more than four thousand feet below the level of the sea. Norway—its grandeur half concealed by the black waters that lie heavily between the somber cliffs—is one of the most marvelous and most inspiring scenic regions of the world.

We made a long twilight ride, down the twisted coils of one of the grandest roads in all the world, a road that leads us down to the Geiranger Fjord, a titanic gorge, filled halfway to the brink with the waters of the wide Atlantic.

Far below lies a lake-like fragment of the sea, deep, dark, eternally quiescent, and yet a living member of the mighty ocean, for it is in reality the tip of a long finger of the sea, crooked round a rocky headland, as if to feel the pulse of this cold Scandinavian land, so recently released from the icy grip of the glaciers, that have now receded upland from the fjords, leaving that little patch of fertile, level earth where pygmy man may play at keeping house in the rude gaards of Merok.

The Geiranger Fjord.

Norway is a land of cleanliness even if modern plumb- ▶
ing is not yet in evidence in the small towns and villages. The traveler is always sure to find decent rooms,
good wholesome food, a cheery welcome, and an honest host in towns like this seaport town, Aalesund.

In the course of a long mountain journey from fjord to
fjord over the famous Grotlid road we spent an hour
on the shores of the Djupvand, a repellent little lake,
half frozen even in mid-summer, where we found
shelter in a comfortable tourist hut established and
supported by the government for the security and
comfort of the traveler. It is a "Fast Skyds Station"—
that is to say, a post where a fixed or "fast" number of
post horses must be kept and where the owner must
provide immediate change of horses on pain of having
fines imposed for all delays exceeding fifteen minutes.

The ponies are admirable little brutes, well fed, well
groomed, and rarely overworked, for the kind-
hearted driver always walks up the ascents, even when
the rise is so gradual that a spirit-level would be required to detect it; and when a steeper grade is
reached, if you do not get out and walk yourself, you
must be prepared to meet the reproachful glance of
the indignant driver. Had I to be born into the animal
kingdom in the course of future transmigrations, I
should pray that my soul might manifest itself in the
form of a petted pony here among these people who
are merciful; and they are as honest with the stranger
as they are kindly to their beasts, and they hold their
honest services so cheap. [See colorplate on page 212]

Not more than one traveler in ten is so fortunate as to see the Midnight Sun from the North Cape. The weather gods of that far northern extremity of Europe are not kind. Far kinder are those that rule the clouds and mists that wander between the seas and skies in the regions near the famous and most lovely of all Norwegian fjords—the Lyngenfjord. Gazing northward from the mouth of that vast Arctic inlet many a thrilled and happy traveler has beheld in all its midnight glory—the golden sun, setting and—without disappearing—rising again to begin another daily course around the Arctic horizon.

▼ Among the dwellers in the Norwegian Nordland there are today some twenty thousand little people of an alien race, the Lapps, wanderers, yet ever wandering over the same desolate no-man's land that lies between the habitable regions of Norway and north Sweden. Reindeer rearing is the favorite occupation of the Lapps, who in the summer pitch their camps near the little Nordland ports to profit by the passing of the tourist.

Like the photograph of the Lapp family, this picture of ▶ Hammerfest was made long after night, or what is called night, had fallen—at nine or ten o'clock P.M. But day and night are terms that have become meaningless; the sun never sinks far enough below the horizon to make much difference in the illumination of the scenes past which we glide as in an endless, sleepless dream. Four hours' sleep each night is more than any of us cared to take. For three days and nights I was practically a stranger to my bunk, remaining dressed all night, snatching a little rest in the lounging rooms upon the upper deck. Every hour brings its incident of interest or its striking vision of sublimity. We have allowed our watches to run down, as useless. Therefore I cannot say what time it was when we approached the little city which of all the cities on earth lies nearest the pole. I think, however, that it was early in the morning that we glided into the harbor of Hammerfest, the midnight sun metropolis, a city of about twenty-five hundred souls. More than two months of darkness is the annual fate of Hammerfest. But for seventy-seven days, from the 13th of May until the 29th of July, the sun swings around the town, rising and falling slightly, but never going out of sight at all, save when it hides behind a hill or house.

From a neighboring height we look down on the almost land-locked harbor, where fishing ships have settled like a flock of gulls on the blue surface of the waters, their white sails spread to catch and hold the light that is so generously shed upon this region by the long summer days, as if in compensation for the sunless days of the past winter.

The Kiss of Judas in the 1910 performance.

1910 OBERAMMERGAU

Once more the world has witnessed the fulfillment of the promise made by the people of Oberammergau three hundred and sixty-seven years ago. Once more the reverent or curious thousands have assembled in the sacred theater that lies within the shadow of the cross-crowned Kofel. Once more the village folk have performed their celebrated Passion Play, the most impressive dramatic presentation of modern times.

Despite the material changes of two decades, the spirit of the Play and of the players remains unchanged. Although a railway now brings worldly crowds to the remote Bavarian hamlet, the drama has not lost its sacred character, the actors have not lost their reverence, nor the people their honesty of purpose. A sojourn among the villagers brings no disillusion to the stranger; instead it brings increased respect and admiration for the unique community of earnest men and women who, every tenth year, emerge from a self-imposed obscurity and offer to the Christian world a marvelous representation of the sublimest tragedy of all time.

Four thousand people are around us, but we forget their presence, and they, too, are far away in the first century, witnesses of this sublimest sacrifice. What their impressions are we cannot tell. We see the tears in many eyes, some sobs are heard; we see faces pale and drawn, and other faces quite unmoved. But even those who see in the picture there revealed nothing but a spectacle, a play, recognize the solemnity and intensity of its import.

The Deposition of Christ in the 1890 performance.

183

SALZBURG

◄ Salzburg is without question the chief show-place of Austria, the most attractive of the Austrian cities, the one most visited by lovers of the picturesque. Mozart was born in Salzburg in 1756. He is the chief celebrity of the city and they keep his memory fresh by means of monuments and tablets and all manner of reminders.

THE AUSTRIAN ALPS

We climbed an hour in the misty darkness that preceded dawn, and found ourselves at sunrise on the ridge, where the fog suddenly forsook us, unveiling all the awful isolation of the ghostly crest on which we stood. We reached the Little Glockner, then scrambled down and crossed that awful place between the peaks; and scaled the white, ice-crested pinnacle of the Big Glockner and stood at last beside the iron cross atop that peak.

There is just room there for the cross—a tall cross, two-thirds of which is now buried in the snow that is heaped five feet deep on the apex of the mountain. And there we stood looking out upon a sea of vapors not less than a full hundred square miles in extent. The whole world had been overwhelmed, submerged and blotted out, save for the rocky tip of the greater Alpine peaks, which now and then thrust themselves above the surface, like the heads of drowning giants struggling in a rush tide.

 ►

▼ My trip to South America had its beginning in Washington, D.C., in the Palace of the Pan-American Union, in the course of a conversation with the director of this new institution.

The "Pan-American Union" is a voluntary organization of the twenty-one American Republics including the United States—maintained by their annual contributions, controlled by a board composed of diplomatic representatives in Washington and the Secretary of State. The marble building with its beautiful open patio, its superb assembly halls and busy offices, cost one million dollars—of which sum three-fourths was donated by that great builder of temples of knowledge and palaces of peace, Andrew Carnegie. President Taft planted the peace tree in the patio, and presided at the dedication this day.

SOUTH AMERICA

It's an awful blow to the Yankee's pride to visit South America. He has regarded it in his ignorance as a land of yellow fever and revolutions. Arriving there, a revolution is inevitable in the mind of the self-styled "American" of North America. He finds that the term "America" embraces about twice as much territory—and about twenty times as many nations as he imagined. He finds South American cities that surpass Paris in beauty, equal London in finish, and rival New York in rush—cities of more than a million inhabitants.

BRAZIL

Rio's beauty is a strange, a unique beauty; in that ▶ beauty there is an uncanny, curiously *impossible* something, difficult to describe, more difficult not to feel and enjoy.

As we stood on the crest of the Corcovado, the "Hunchback Mountain" that rises two thousand feet and more above the Bay of Rio, and bends over the fair city as in a zealously protecting stoop, we looked down in delighted amazement to the scene outspread below. Unlike all other panoramas, queerer and grander than all, strangely unnatural and yet replete with natural beauty. "What do you think of it?" I ask the friend who had stood with me at so many famous points of view during our nineteen years of picture-taking, picture-seeking travel. "Well," he replies, "now I can understand the feelings of the old farmer who when first he set eyes on a giraffe gazed fixedly at the unfamiliar 'critter,' so unlike the horses, cows, and pigs of his own experience, and then declared slowly and with conviction, but without taking his eyes from the long-necked foreign thing, 'There ain't no such animal.'"

So the traveler who stands on Corcovado and surveys the Bay of Rio and its weirdly wonderful surroundings is tempted to paraphrase the exclamation of that astonished farmer and affirm, deliberately, ungrammatically, and with sincerity, "There ain't no such scenery."

Manaus, with its waterfront activity, reminded me of similar Mississippi port scenes I'd seen: a flurry of dock people and riverboats paddling to a not-so-subtle mercantile rhythm. [See colorplate on page 213]

THE ANDES

An amusing incident occurred on our trip to the Andes, worth the telling. We had a letter of introduction to the superintendent of the narrow-gauge line called the Transandino—an Englishman—like nearly all the men who boss the big jobs in this part of the world. We explained our photographic mission. "Good advertising!" he exclaimed, "I will put the Presidential Sofa on the morning train." The Presidential Sofa is an Andean institution. When not in use it adorns the anteroom of the superintendent's office. When in use it is securely clamped to the cowcatcher of a restive locomotive that takes to the Transandino trail of steel like an untamed mustang and now and then gives imitations of a bucking bronco as it hits the rough spots or rounds the sudden, unexpected curves. They keep that sofa for the use of South American Presidents, Diplomatic Representatives, British shareholders, and other distinguished travelers, including motion-picture men whose right to a satisfying survey of the scenery is not to be denied.

There is no lack of motion in the motion picture that we make in the course of our seven-hour dash up into the heart of the Andean Cordillera. Almost at once, as we approach the mountains, all vegetation vanishes. We are soon in a glaring desert with savage dolmen-like peaks rearing themselves on all sides. Farther on the colors of the scene are red, white, and blue—red rocks, white sunshine, and blue sky. Then suddenly the color scheme will change again as our engine rounds a bend, nearly flinging us out of our sofa and revealing to our tired and dazzled eyes peaks of different tones and shapes and valley vistas of unutterable vastness and unspeakable barrenness and scenes of glorious gloom. We climb much faster than we imagined possible. It is like trying to keep track of the changes in a kaleidoscope while shooting the chutes uphill in a boat that now and then forgets to shoot and "bumps the bumps" instead. Meanwhile we are making motion pictures of every striking section of the line—and if you can imagine yourselves clinging to that Presidential Sofa on the cowcatcher of that prancing locomotive as it dashes along this colorful line you may be able to gather some impression of what we saw in those seven eventful hours.

ARGENTINA (The Cataracts of the Iguassú)

The Iguassú lies far from the haunts and highways of modern man. Never did a destination appear more elusive than the Iguassú appeared to us; we did not know it would ultimately cost us twenty-seven days of strenuous travel and precarious toil. Our party consisted of four English and two American travelers determined to "discover" the falls, but unable to get any really definite information about them in Buenos Aires. Some people told us we could do the Iguassú trip easily in fourteen days; others said two or three months would be the time required. Some said that the mosquitoes would eat us alive and that the tropic heat would prove deadly; others said that we should surely die of cold. One man assured me that the trip would cost five hundred dollars gold; another said that his stenographer had spent an economical vacation at the falls.

We resolved ourselves in the Anglo-American "Missouri Society" and started out prepared to let the railway and the river steamboat people "show us" how much they didn't know about the country traversed by their lines. We were able on our return to report to them that their advertising folders, with outlines of the tour, giving hours of arrival and departure and details about rail and boat connections all set down in clearest black and white, represented the best "comic literature" we had ever perused. Nothing happened as therein promised and predicted. What happened was never on the program—and therefore doubly interesting and amusing—at least to those of us who carried the spirit of the real traveler into the terra incognita of the Upper Paraná.

The start, however, was very promising. The sleeping-car train in which we made the first stage of the journey northward from Buenos Aires to Concordia was the best equipped that we had seen in Argentina. One interesting feature of the run was a four-hour ferry transfer from port to port on the Paraná River. An all-steel car ferry took the entire train aboard and bore it grandly up the majestic river for nearly half a hundred miles.

Beyond Concordia a new railway carried us, with many delays and uncertainties, across a very raw, new-looking country. The scenery is—well, it is "Pampaesque"—straight horizon, no trees; nothing but telegraph poles. One novel detail only—the innumerable nests built of mud by the ovenbird on nearly every telegraph pole along the entire line. Where the ovenbird built its nests before the telegraph poles grew from this treeless pampa is a puzzle!

We had been warned to be very careful when visiting the little Paraguayan port of Villa Encarnación, across the river from Posadas, not to wander far from the landing, for fear of being carried off and wedded forcibly against our will. We thought this was all said in jest. But our first experience on shore was an invitation from the widowed mother of six daughters to enter their humble home and "*Tomar maté*"—that is, take a sip of Paraguayan tea. Wise mothers never overlook an opportunity. It might just happen that the black eyes of one or another of the six señoritas might do their work and win a son-in-law for a family, the personnel of which is now hopelessly feminine.

At last we learn of the belated arrival of the river boat for which we have waited four days at Posadas and on which we must now spend four days more ascending the Upper Paraná. After many long days, we reach Puerto Aguirre, at which tourists for the Iguassú must disembark, our steamer turns aside from the Paraná and runs a mile or less up a tributary stream which is the Iguassú itself, down which the waters from the cataracts make their way to the larger river.

The "Grand Hotel del Iguassú" was a disappointment. The proprietor said that it was "in liquidation." Whenever anyone fell through the broken-down front steps, he chuckled "liquidación," as if the incident consoled him for the money he had lost in the thankless task of providing comforts, or what he thinks are comforts, for travelers who never, never come. The total of tourists who have thus far visited the cataracts is a mere handful—a meager hundred or two each year. No wonder Don Leandro has become a sort of quizzical misanthrope and that he chuckles "liquidación" when his tourists skin their shins on his front steps. Sometimes the river rises to the level of his inelegant veranda. I am told that one year the water stood five feet deep in his dining room, the river having risen suddenly.

Don Leandro is also in charge of the transportation system. He has twenty mules to feed and thirteen miles of trail through a tropic forest to keep clear—a never-ending hopeless proposition. We followed this exquisite but rough trail for thirteen lovely miles. We rode as through an endless tropical conservatory, attended by a troop of gorgeous butterflies that formed halos of colored glory round our heads. It was a ride to be remembered—the pleasure of it enhanced by the thought that we did not have to travel in Don Leandro's coach and six, in which our fellow touristas elected to make the pilgrimage. We let the lumbering coché rattle on ahead. We followed in the saddle at a walk in the silence of the orchid-laden forest—with our faithful butterflies winging with us like a kaleidoscopic cloud. It was a charming preparation for the glorious scene that rewarded our wanderings.

At last we came to the hotel—Don Leandro's annex that overlooks the falls, but with a remoteness from them that is disappointing. You must not judge the Iguassú at first glance. To travelers who go no nearer than their comfort and their safety counsel, the Iguassú offers no thrill—nothing but a pretty view of a very distant waterfall. Therefore, suspending judgment, we enter the hotel and register. That is, we tack our cards upon the wooden wall. Lucky that tourists do not arrive at night—they could not register without waking all the other guests. Then we pick our camp beds and make ourselves at home. It never occurred to Don Leandro, who has himself brought the twelve tourists here today, that they might want to eat and drink during their stay. He has brought no bread, no meat, no beer, no wine—never thought of it—no wonder both hotels are in "liquidación"! Happily we have all brought canned food of some kind and there's lots of fresh water to drink from the falls, the lesser ones so near the hotel that every evening we washed the films we had developed in the eddying pools upon the brink. But the grander falls are so far away as to give us a first shock of disappointment. We realize at once that to see the Iguassú Falls at close range will be the task of many days and call for much rough work. We spent eight never-to-be forgotten days in photographing the falls from the many hard-won points of view to which we found or forced our way.

We photographed the roaring cataracts, the graceful cascades, and the ethereal falls. The coloring of the Iguassú is wonderful. The rocks are of a rich chocolate brown, framed by all the deep and gorgeous greens of an almost equatorial forest. We saw scenes of overwhelming life and energy!

Each night, after a hard day of picture-making, my companion, the indefatigable Depue, would set to work with his developing machine and his tanks, bottles, and chemicals, set out in the moonlight on a tiny island in the stream just above the cascade nearest to the shanty where we lodged. There was no lack of cool, clean, flowing water for the washing of the films. A portable rack facilitated the drying of the long strips of negative so that when we left this remote spot and started back toward civilization we had stowed in our kit, neatly reeled and tightly sealed, a fifteen-hundred-foot film record of the sights that we had seen in the course of our eight days of scrambling over rocks, canoeing through rapids, creeping out to the edge of misty precipices, and wading waist deep from isle to isle across the rushing channels of the Upper Iguassú.

To see the full glory of the Great Falls we must spend still another day, aided by the two Indian guides, cruising precariously in the smaller of the two dug-out canoes—working our way far enough upstream to slide in safety across the stronger currents to the shelter of a little group of islands hovering on the very brink of the abyss, called La Garganta del Diablo, or The Devil's Throat. Into that throat the main current of the river is apparently sucked by the thirsty diablo. One little ledge of rock projects far enough to give our cameras a "down-look" into the misty deeps. The scene is indescribable, as are all scenes of supreme grandeur. Pictures fail to convey to one who has not stood here any conception of the wonder and beauty of it all.

We are loath to leave our mist-drenched island in the brink. We know that our eyes are looking upon no common hackneyed, tourist-ridden sight. So few white men have ever looked upon this scene that it might almost be said that it is a sight unknown to the world whence we have come. For centuries the waters of the Iguassú have thundered here unheard, unseen, save by the unimpressionable native Indians of earlier

Machu Picchu.

ages—and in our time by the few adventurous white men who have come to look, to marvel, and then to retrace their way out from the dense primeval forest and down the silent, unfrequented river to the frontiers of an advancing civilization which creeps but very slowly toward the spot where we are standing now. But the white man has noted the power as well as the beauty and the glory of the Iguassú. That power he will some day seize for his own purposes—for the lightening of the labors of humankind. May he, at the same time, fail not to respect the beauty and the glory of the Iguassú—for the joy of the human eye and for the uplifting of the human soul.

PERU

The high walls of Cuzco were built by Viracocha, an Inca ruler of the fifteenth century. Like the fortress-city of Machu Picchu, the walls and ruins sum up the enigma of the Incas: how and whence they came to be constructed. Fragments—caught in an ancient wisp of time, rarefied but not forgotten.

1912 HAVANA

We chanced to reach Havana just before the second sinking of the "Maine," the formal burial of the battered hulk which had just been raised, after being submerged for many years. She had been literally cut in two by the explosion of her magazines, caused by the

Havana

Raising the
USS "Maine."

Coffins with bodies recovered from the "Maine."

explosion of a mine placed by wretches, still unknown, beneath the forward portion of her hull.

The work of lifting the old "Maine" has lasted eighteen months, but finally she floats again, triumphantly, to unfurl new flags above the scene of her assassination. All this labor, time, and money has been spent in order that Uncle Sam may give his brave old ship, at last, a decent burial.

More than two hundred and sixty victims perished when the "Maine" went down. The bodies of some were not recovered until the "Maine" was raised, thirteen years after the catastrophe. All rest now in our National Cemetery, near Washington, with the main mast of the "Maine" standing as their monument above their graves. So vanishes for all time the gallant ship whose tragic fate so materially changed the destinies of our United States.

BUILDING THE PANAMA CANAL

The task of cutting South America adrift there at the narrow isthmus by means of which it hangs to our own continent has been almost completed—a few months more and our great sister continent will be an independent island. Then, perhaps, when South America has become geographically, as well as politically, a foreign country, we may begin to take an interest in her destiny—in her civilization, in the sights to be seen, and in the lessons to be learned. Travel to and through South America will certainly receive a tremendous impetus with the completion of the Panama Canal.

By studying these pictures you can get some vague conception of the enterprise, the ingenuity, the daring, and the wealth of Uncle Sam.

◄ Behind all the machines, that do man's bidding with a million times man's power, are over forty thousand working men of many nationalities. Here is a group of Spaniards; but you will find in Panama men of all races and all nations, doing the world's work well.

1913 THE PHILIPPINES

It has taken us a six-day hike to get here to beautiful Bontoc—the Igorot metropolis. It lies on a treacherous, capricious river, three thousand feet above the sea. We are amazed to find this remote, chief city of the Igorots already so conspicuously Americanized. The things that have followed our flag are legion. The Bontoc Bilibid, the model prison for the correction of the head-hunting mania. And the new hospital, where they do everything for the Igorots except the putting on of heads that have been cut off. Here we find a doctor from Milwaukee, and nurses from northern Illinois.

At the Provincial Government building we are received by the Governor, who orders out his Igorot constabulary to show us what a splendid military force can be recruited from these superb natives. The Governor speaks the Igorot dialect and orders these men out in their own language—and very little else! The hat, the "G" string and cartridge belt (and sometimes, a shirt) make up the uniform of these beautiful, bronze Bontoc boys. Don't think they have stripped to have their picture taken. They are fully, properly clad.

The old men of Bontoc still preserve with pride, trophies of their youthful prowess in the head-hunting game. It was, so to speak, the National Game of the Igorots. Five skulls, taken only a few years ago, were brought out by the Mayor of the town from the old men's council house. Today, head-hunting is almost obsolete, punishable with life imprisonment. It was too much a recognized heroic custom, a necessary proof of valor, a token of a petty but proud patriotism, to be treated as a capital offense. Our judges have been humane and wise enough to put themselves in our brown brother's place and see things from his primitive point of view. And happily this policy of common sense is succeeding. There is more murder today in New York City or Chicago than head-hunting in all the primitive wildernesses of Luzon.

INDIA

From every point of view the Taj Mahal is perfect in both symmetry and beauty. With other buildings we must occupy a certain point of view to see them at their best. But this miraculous creation is always and from every point of view perfectly balanced—correctly composed. We cannot throw it out of line or of proportion by standing at unfavorable points of view. There are no wrong spots at which to stand, no angles adverse to a satisfying survey of the Taj. Perfect within, perfect without, perfect in line and color and design, and better than all else, perfect in motive and sentiment; for the one was grateful love, the other was life-long affection.

The Taj Mahal, the Oriental pendant to the Grecian Parthenon, as perfect in design as the world-famous masterpiece of the Greek Age of glory, but far more beautiful, and unlike the Parthenon, not a ruin, but intact in its surpassing beauty unmarred by war's disasters, untarnished by the stains of time, white, pure and perfect as when the last conscientious toiler took away his tools, leaving behind him the most beautiful building on the face of our revolving globe.

203

The Ganges is one of the world's most amazing sights—this riverfront of the holy city at the hour when the population and the pilgrims come to perform their ancient rights, as they have been performed here almost without change for at least three thousand years.

I was not totally prepared for the most amazing and repellent sight in the world as I approached the old Hindu city of Benares on the banks of the all-holy river called the Ganges.

To LIVE in Benares is to every pious Hindu a high and holy privilege.

To DIE in Benares on the shore of this most sacred river is to gain instant entrance into the Paradise of Siva.

To BATHE in the turgid waters of the Ganges is to wash away all trace of carnal sin.

To PERFORM here the many, long-enduring, complex, and mysterious religious rites practiced by the Brahmin is to cleanse the soul of all impurities and to prepare it to return perfected into the all-embracing one-ness of the infinite essence where alone dwells perfect peace.

But this royal road to ultimate peace and joy appears to those of us not numbered among the elect as a most distressing highroad to the hereafter, frequented by the tumultuous mob of frenzied seekers after salvation. [See colorplate on page 214]

The Taj Mahal.

A festival in Rangoon.

BURMA

Beautiful Burma! The loveliest land of England's Oriental Empire. The land is Buddhist, the people gentle, cheerful, and in contrast to the religion-obsessed races of the Indian peninsula, delightfully human, approachable, congenial. To the traveler, stunned by the overwhelming splendors and oppressed by the equally overwhelming squalor of India itself, a little ramble in this land of lightheartedness, among peoples of a gentler faith and even quainter customs, serves as a delightful "after cure." [See also colorplate on page 215]

The Pyramids, Egypt, 1906.

Twins walking past the Opera House, Vienna, 1907.

In a Paris park, 1907.

Horse post station, Norway, 1909.

The port of Manaus, Brazil, 1911.

At an Indian festival, 1913.

Bathing in the Ganges, India, 1913.

The Taj Mahal, India, 1913.

A reclining Buddha, Burma, 1913.

Castle Combe village, England, 1914.

I have come to study living London, to see what manner of life is lived in the London of today; and so we come to Piccadilly Circus to watch the world go by—the commonplace world of which we are a part, but a world which becomes wonderful the moment that we are content to step aside and for a space become merely spectators of its everyday doings.

The passings and repassings of the myriad buses; the ceaseless crossings and intercrossings of the human millions is one of the most impressive things in London—one difficult to picture, for in a picture we do not feel the endlessness of the procession.

◀ There is no monotony in the feast of beauty that is spread before the traveler in rural England. The exquisitely finished aspect of the country, the absence of industrial scars, the picturesqueness of the old-time towns and villages make touring a delight.

Ireland is rich—rich in many things that richer nations lack. Ireland is rich in beauty, rich in pride of race, in devotion to religion, and in a fearless hopefulness that the worst misfortunes cannot kill.

To one who does not know the beautiful green island whence have come our many Irish fellow-citizens, their love and admiration for their native isle may appear strange. Why should they love a country where their fathers suffered? What affection do they owe to

Buggy drivers wait at the station to take guests to local hotels.

▲ poor old Ireland, always pictured to us as a distressful country, as a land of poverty and woe? Yet go to Ireland—look upon her beauty, realize her wealth of possibilities, feel the cheering warmth of Irish welcome, treat your eyes to Irish smiles, your ears to Irish wit; let the simple sincerity of Irish life reveal to you the unsuspected depths of Irish character and you will understand why Irishmen love Ireland, and you, too, will often turn with loving and regretful glances toward the beautiful, unhappy island that lies so near to England—and yet so far away—if distance is measured by mutual understanding.

Among the holy sites in Ireland none is dearer to the ▶ pious patriot than the great Rock of Cashel in County Tipperary. A holy place it has been for a thousand years and more, in spite of the tradition concerning the infernal origin of the rock itself. Ask any old-time Tipperary man how it came there, and he will tell you how long years ago the devil took a big bite out of the crest of a neighboring range of mountains, and how finding the mouthful very dry and tough he spat it out upon the floor of Ireland's fairest valley.

In proof of this they show you this isolated Rock of Cashel, and a great gap in the skyline of a mountain

several miles away. The buildings on the rock are in many ways remarkable. There is a beautiful cathedral, beautifully ruined, a castle admirably fallen to decay, and a little Norman church known as King Cormac's Chapel. There is, of course, an Irish tower, round as a rod and wonderfully well preserved, and there are Irish crosses, one so old and worn that it is nearly formless; and there is also a modern copy of an ancient cross that shows us what those splendid monuments were like before the tooth of time had gnawed into their quaintly cut designs.

And round about there is a view unrivaled in its verdant richness, for from this height you can look out on the Golden Vale of Tipperary, as sweet a vale as green grass ever grew in. In this rich valley lies the celebrated "Golden Vein" of Irish soil—the richest and most fertile in all Ireland.

◄ We have a train to catch—and such a train!—the queerest, most absurd, most utterly outlandish train that we have ever seen. Its name, too, is appropriately outlandish; it is the "Ballybunnion Mono-Rail Express." It runs from a station on the ordinary line to Ballybunnion, about ten miles away on the Atlantic Coast. It runs upon a single elevated rail, a mono-rail, astride of which a double locomotive, or rather one shaped like a pair of bloomers, hauls a train of cars that likewise ride the mono-rail on wheels which are concealed in the long slot with which the Ballybunnion Limited is slit from stem to stern. To enable passengers to cross over to the compartments on the other side, there is one car that is nothing but a sort of stile like those by means of which one gets over fences in the country. The track itself is like a metal fence, ten miles in length. The line is spanned by bridges with a double draw that can be let down by the peasants when they wish to drive their carts or cows across.

Get a horse!"

221

The speed of this peculiar railway, although not surpassing seven miles an hour, nevertheless exceeds that of the only competing conveyances in the form of tiny two-wheeled carts, drawn by donkeys, driven by dignified old dames.

_____

There on the summit of the cliff we see what seems ▶ to be an old baronial castle and we wonder what rich and happy noble dwells on this noble height and looks out every day upon this noble view. With envious steps we make our way along the brink toward that superbly perched chateau, hoping perchance to find the lord and lady of the manor on the terrace surveying this glorious estate of earth and sea and sky. But we found upon the threshold not just the sort of group that we had pictured! A small herd of cows was placidly ruminating there. Sadly, we turned away from the old O'Brian Tower, now become the "Castle of the Cows," for we were sad to think that men would let these beauty-blind and unappreciative brutes usurp for their dull, uninspired uses so glorious a site—one fit for the castle of an artist or a king.

_____

◀ Edinburgh Castle looms high above the old town and the new. It is one of the great sights of the world, one of those things that stamp themselves forever in the memory. It is superb from every point of view. It seems to rise like some citadel of medieval romance in lonely, frowning isolation—even as we view it from the busy confusion and modernity of Princes Street.

It was upon the easily defended summit of the Castle Rock that some early chieftain of some barbarous, prehistoric clan must have reared the first crude stockade under the protection of which his people built the mud and fagot hovels of the village to which centuries later Edwin, King of the invading Northumbrians, gave the name of "Edwin's Burgh"—whence the "Edinburgh" of today.

▲ It is a pleasing, and certainly not an unprofitable, occupation for the tourist to sit at his hotel window, on Princes Street, and watch the lingering twilight of the north climb up Castle Rock, and finally, leave it in the care of Night, as it has done, day after day, so many million times since a caprice of Nature placed it there. The Gothic spire in the background is Scott's Monument, Edinburgh's tribute to pure literary genius in Sir Walter Scott.

THE WORLD GROWS SMALLER

1915–1938

"Nirvana," the Holmes apartment on Central Park West.

1915 NEW YORK CITY

Some day I will attempt a lecture on New York City, a subject no lecturer possessed of half an eye or half a tongue could really fail to put across to an audience.

Thinking thus, I gaze from my own apartment windows which look down on Central Park. I see beyond that spacious playground, Fifth Avenue—that richest of all thoroughfares—along its upper reaches rise the palaces of men who are rich beyond the dreams of Croesus. There rise cliff-dwellings of innumerable stones, to dwell in which small families pay rentals of thirty thousand dollars for a twenty-room apartment. The great hotels clustered around the Plaza glow like towering fairy palaces on fire—and the honks of motors, the rich music of Rolls-Royces and the squeak of Fords—the rattle of dilapidated trolley cars—the sirens of the fire engines—and the roar of neighboring Broadway—rise in a soft confused, confusing and to me a fascinating murmur. Who in all the world would not be thrilled by such a sight as this. [See colorplate on page 242]

226

ON THE ROAD IN AMERICA

A quarter of a century of travel has shown me the wonders of nearly all the world. The spell of foreign travel has always been upon me—the impelling motive of my life and work. Yet I know that were all other lands to perish, or like Atlantis sink into the sea, the traveler who seeks the inspiration of beauty and grandeur, of romance and antiquity, need not in any way despair, for he would find within the borders of our own United States an exhaustless wealth of charm and wonder—ample compensation for his lost lands of delight.

What we most lack here in America are not the great things that grip the traveler's attention; our land is replete with wonderful sights of the first magnitude. What we lack are the thousand and one little touches of comfort and convenience that European nations know so well how to provide. First of all, good roads; then, first of all also, the little things that charm the traveler, little luxuries, courtesies, and comforts that cast a halo of delight about our days in Italy or England, or Germany or Switzerland.

But those who cater to the traveler here in America are making a beginning. In many places a broad-minded effort has been made to make the traveler feel that all our splendid railway systems and our big hotels exist for his enjoyment. In the old days the traveler used to be made to think that he existed primarily for their profit.

THE PANAMA-PACIFIC EXPOSITION IN SAN FRANCISCO

A thing of beauty is a joy forever. Even though all the buildings of the Panama-Pacific Exposition are ephemeral structures, doomed to disappear within a year, the Exposition being a thing of perfect beauty will remain a joy forever in the memory of all who were so fortunate as to go to San Francisco in 1915.

There is a thrill in the thought that all the wonder and beauty of this Exposition are really only a spontaneous manifestation of the world's admiration for the works of those great soldiers of progress and all the humble workers to whose genius and energy we owe the Panama Canal.

Before us looms the commanding mass of what may be called the gate of honor of the Exposition, the arch upon which rests the most conspicuous feature of the architectural scheme, the tower with its thousands of scintillating gems. The arch is noble, but the tower is unworthy of the Roman pedestal on which it stands. It is a freakish thing, novel and expositional, but without dignity or real impressiveness. It is an architectural curio that barely escapes the epithet grotesque. The worst thing about it is the fact that it has been so praised by those who like it simply because it is so big and so conspicuous and because they don't know any better, and because it cost five hundred thousand dollars. It is four hundred and thirty-three feet high. It

A mural painter and his handiwork.

was to have been one hundred feet higher, but even an Exposition must economize somewhere, and the tower design was the victim of a reduced appropriation. Had not its skyward aspirations been arrested by base material consideration, the Tower of Jewels might have realized in beauty and impressiveness the ideal that was in the mind of Thomas Hastings when he conceived his more ambitious plan.

By night, the Tower of Jewels comes into its own and easily eclipses all else within the gates. Transfigured by the floods of light poured up at it from countless hidden sources, it seems to stretch in dignified immensity and endlessness into the upper air, becoming, under the magic influence of the searchlights' glare, a thing of beauty with a compelling personality that justifies the dominating place it holds. As the lights change the jewels glitter and glisten as if myriads of stars, attracted by all this unwonted burst of brilliancy and color, had descended from the heavens and massed themselves there on the terraces and amid the columns, like heavenly spectators of an earthly carnival.

230

The great arch frames a striking picture of architectural glory and monumental grace against a background of the black, star-deserted sky. Crossed rapiers of incandescent light are touching the figure of the heroic spirit of Man there upon the capital of the Pillar of Progress.

▼ The building in the foreground is the Spanish Renaissance style Varied Industries Palace. In the background, the Tower of Jewels.

Loveliest of all, perhaps, is the Palace of Fine Arts. ▼ Someone has called this wonderful building "a realized dream, imagined irrespective of time, cost, or demand." It must have come to Maybeck, the architect, in a vision. It rises there upon the curving shores of a lagoon, too beautiful, too splendid to be real. It is beautiful at all hours of the day, under all manner of conditions. The fogs which sweep in almost daily from the bay give it an added charm, the vague charm of a beautiful mystery half revealed and half obscured.

231

1916 C A N A D A

▲ As a rule a big hotel in a beautiful mountain region is the one blot on the landscape, but here at Banff the architect has handled his design supremely well. He has made his hotel the keynote of a superb situation, not only an admirable but a necessary feature of the view. Without the Banff Springs Hotel the scenery of Banff would lack something that seems essential: a focal point, a central rallying point for the eye, an ideal teeing place from which to make your visual drive over the scenic links of one of Nature's most alluring courses.

Lake Louise is the loveliest lake in Canada, if not in all ▶ the world. No picture can fully satisfy the eye that has once looked upon Louise. Tears of delight come into many eyes at first sight of all this overwhelming beauty. I have seen such tears, even if I did not shed them.

Nature sets this spectacle of beauty here before us and the response it wakens in our souls proves that we are each one of us possessed of the artistic instinct, that if we will but yield to it, a love of beauty can and will control, console and bless our earthly love.

1917 AUSTRALIA

▲ The civic center of Sydney is in Martin Place, a short wide street upon which front the finest buildings of the city. If anything happens in Sydney, it is sure to be in Martin Place. The recruiting campaign found here its logical headquarters. Here every day at noon vast crowds were harangued with soul-stirring appeals to enlist and save the Empire.

———————

Reading the signs in the streets of a strange city is ofttimes interesting. I regret I did not sample the fare ▲ of the Chicago Dining and Tea Room, where the prices appeared so moderate and the place so cozy and quiet.

———————

The governing hand of the white man now holds the ▶ aboriginal race in close subjection to his will. The coming of the white man with his ships and guns and gospels was the beginning of the end of the isolated Australian aborigine.

▲ The building with a central heating plant is almost unknown in Australia. The shivering visitor has the option of paying for a fire that won't burn or an electric heater which merely looks hot and does not heat. Keeping warm in Australia is a purely personal obligation, something to be attended to at your own expense, something that is no concern of the hotel proprietor nor of the owner of a building.

I went one evening to a concert in the grandiose town hall of Sydney; as I entered the huge concert auditorium, I thought that the entire audience was smoking. It was not. It was merely breathing! What I thought was smoke puffed from a thousand lips was merely the breath made visible by the low temperature. Nobody seemed to mind—ladies in evening dress snuggled into their heavy wraps—men kept their ulsters on—I turned my collar up and wished that I had brought a steamer rug. I began to understand why the Russian pianist pounded the piano so hard; he, too, was trying to keep warm.

236

I asked where I could see the kangaroo in its native state. Nothing is easier, I found, if you do not mind a rail journey and a rough ride in a motorcar through the bush and out upon the inland plains of South Australia, where the adventurous sportsmen of Adelaide go now and then to hunt the wild marsupial from motor cars. The proposition promises excitement—and the promise is usually fulfilled. [See colorplate on page 244]

NEW ZEALAND

◄ The Maoris were here hundreds of years before the white man came, living superbly vital lives, conducting tribal warfare as an art and as a duty. Performing ceremonies of immemorial antiquity, training their bodies to be strong, their souls brave in the fray, their nerves to be fearless of pain, defiant of torture. The crude sword-cuts of Heidelberg culture are as nothing compared to the exquisite torture endured in acquiring the fully tattooed face. This is not mere tattooing, it is incised sculpture, the design being literally cut in the flesh, then colored a deep blue.

◄ The famous guides, Georgina and Eileen, their tattooed faces familiar to every tourist, adorn all the best sellers in the picture postcard shops of Rotorua. Each wears suspended like a scapulary a curious little greenstone image, like a contorted Billiken, called a Tiki.

Here's a Wellington idea worthy of our attention. The ►
cable cars offer an admirable arrangement of the seats, preventing what has so often happened in San Francisco, where, when the cable car starts up the hill, one slides gracefully into some unfamiliar lap.

The Wellington railroad station.

It's in the blood, the blood of all of us, the germ that comes down to us from the fighting beast, the fighting germ that makes us heroes, the lack of it making us cowards.

Therefore we cannot blame our brothers or ourselves because we have it or we have it not. Each man must live and act and speak according to the spirit that is in him. I am for peace at any price, save at the cost of honor, real honest honor, not what the diplomatic world calls honor. And yet I give my admiration to the men who, without counting cost or asking any reason why, answer a country's call to arms and do their duty as their courage and their nature makes them see it. [See colorplate on page 241]

It was not easy for civilians to get permits to go abroad in 1918; it was harder still to get permits to carry cameras. But after weeks of effort we wangled the necessary approvals, and permission to sail on the old White Star Liner "Lapland" late in May, when the Germans were within a few miles of Paris.

The Atlantic crossing was not the kind I had been accustomed to. No cheering crowds, no reporters, no unauthorized persons allowed to pass beyond the wire fence that stretched along the waterfront. We kissed our wives goodbye—and I, for one, kissed myself goodbye at the same spot. I definitely expected never to return alive. The "Lapland" with us on board lay there for two days and nights. There appeared to be few passengers. Then suddenly one morning, without sound of whistle or of shouted orders, the ship gently came to life. We were at last on our way to the front. So few of us!

But, as we cleared our pier and looked northward along the Hudson shores, we saw ship after ship, as far as the eye could reach, slowly backing out of other slips.

It began to dawn upon us that we were part of a vast convoy! I had been led to believe that we were to travel on an inoffensive merchant ship with less than a hundred passengers. There were more than that on board. Once out of sight of land—or at least beyond the reach of spying spy-glasses in the high windows of Manhattan's skyscrapers—where many a friend of the enemy kept tabs upon ship movements to and from the

No unofficial touring is allowed in war-time France. ▼ We have our "carnet d'essence"—our little booklet, authorizing us to draw essence or gasoline from any French or Yankee supply station anywhere in France. To get essence from a French depot is a task that taxes time and temper, so complex the formalities, so slow the service, so antiquated the methods of supply. But when you strike a Yankee depot—show your card— sign your slip—grab your gas and on your way!

An observation balloon and an aerial photo taken from it.

port—once out in the open spaces of the Atlantic, suddenly up from between decks came a roaring, cheering khaki-colored flood of doughboys, twenty-two hundred of them! During the two days and nights of waiting at the pier, we had no inkling of their presence. Now our decks were all awash with howling saviors of Democracy on their way to deal with the Kaiser's armies "over there." The decks of all the other liners had at the same time taken on a khaki-colored tinge. There were more than twenty-three thousand soldiers of the American Expeditionary Force crossing the ocean with us! We were fair game for German U-boats—I wanted to go home.

I had always hated war, feared danger, and disliked discomfort—always prided myself on being a peace-loving, civilized individual. I was already too old for military service as well as lacking physical strength and intestinal fortitude. I just didn't want to get mixed up in the Great War.

Our time in Italy was short. The ways of the authorities were long. We hoped that our permits to visit the zone of actual hostilities would be issued in time. We waited. We tried to see the sights of Florence but sight-seeing in wartime seems a waste of effort.

At last word came that our little party might proceed to the front. From anxious Florence to Bologna where a car, less elegant, was placed at our disposal for our dash to the flaming front. We lost no time along the way. Through beautiful Ferrara and other north Italian cities we sped on and entered Padua, which had become Italian headquarters for the war. It was still intact despite frequent bombings by the enemy. We found lodgings in a hotel where to our surprise an old friend greeted us. Jimmy Hare, the famous war photographer, had established himself in the basement, whence he sent to the American press pictures freshly made in the course of his frequent visits to the nearby fighting lines. Jimmy was perfectly at home in any war zone.

We got our first taste of the real thing that very night. It was a lovely moonlit night—the kind that raiding aviators love, the kind of night that made the populace of Padua wish that no moon was in the sky.

We were told that the first sign of alarm would be the cutting off of all electric lights in town. But the evening passed without alarm. Then, as we prepared to lay us down to rest, suddenly out went every bulb in the hotel and every bulb in town. Then a siren screamed like a vociferous virago in hot anger and in awful fear. We, new to this sort of thing, rushed to the window and then to the house-top to see what we might see. We saw first a star-shell, sent up by the Italians, bursting in high air—as beautiful a burst as one could ask for in any fireworks display. I made an excellent picture of it with the dome of the cathedral faintly outlined below the bright but evanescent bomb-burst. Then after a long period of stilly silence, the real show began: crash and explosion of bombs until the total reached the number of thirteen. All fell in the city—some seemed to fall very near to where we stood on the hotel roof. No people visible in the streets. All had gone down into the air-raid refuges or into any cellar that seemed to promise safety. It never occurred to us to seek shelter—the "courage" of the inexperienced is astonishing.

We heard distant clang of ambulances: then silence. But not for long. The raiders, having corrected their range, began a second attack. Their first bomb literally bounced me out of bed. I thought that it had struck the house; it really landed on another some two blocks away. Others fell, exploded around about. Again the clang of ambulances and a sudden silence. Then something strange and uncanny happened. Although it was only half past two A.M. the dawn came up like a golden glory in the *west*! That golden glow crept around to north and south; it grew brighter and brighter and soon had spread around the entire horizon as if a hundred suns were about to rise on all sides of the city. It seemed as if Nature had lost control of the heavens. We gazed entranced at that mysterious illumination. We simply could not account for it.

When morning came, at last, we learned that what had mystified us was a new form of air raid defense—a fog of light sent up by some new sort of Bengal fires set in a great circle all around the city, screening everything in a haze of foggy luminosity and at the same time making high-flying aircraft visible.

All the next day I studied in amazed horror what had happened where the bombs had fallen. The ruin was appalling. Houses ripped apart, the metal shutters which protect shop windows—long blocks of them, bulging out—a new Ford car which I had been shown proudly by its owner two days before was no longer in the court-yard of the house where he had stored it and the house itself was no longer there.

This was a British tank. The Germans captured it— ▼ painted their cross upon it and sent it back against this labyrinth of trenches. It climbed triumphantly like this, only to fall a second later upon the helpless bodies of the French defenders—a well-placed shell—a direct hit—struck it a fatal blow. "Killed in action" would be a fitting epitaph for this gigantic fighting brute of living steel.

The Vanderbilt mansion with the Plaza Hotel in the background, New York, 1915.

San Francisco Exposition, 1915.

Light creates beauty.

The railroad station in Sydney, Australia, 1917.

Port Philip Bay, Melbourne, Australia, 1917.

Kangaroo hunting.

Slave girls at the coronation of the Emperor Haile Selassie, 1930.

The beach at Biarritz, 1924.

The Blue Grotto, Capri, 1924.

Spain, 1928.

▲ In Metz, we found the children of Lorraine waving once more the dear forbidden flag of France and crying "Vive la France!"

It is difficult to visualize in a picture a state of mind and heart such as we find in this land of Teuton speech and Gallic sympathies, but something of the atmosphere can be seen in the crowds around the empty memorial pedestals. On this one stood King Frederick William III. How much Metz loved him is indicated by what Metz did to his monument in 1918.

Children playing near the ruins of the Cloth Hall.

1919 BELGIUM

Sad as is the violated countryside, beaten to barrenness by the tempest of war, sadder still is the appearance of the cities, devastated by the same man-made storm. Nothing would be left of the martyred town of Ypres, were it not for signs, set near the ruins of St. Martin's Church and the Cloth Hall, which say, "This is Holy Ground. No Stone of this fabric may be taken away. It is a Heritage for all civilized peoples." For the type of civilized people, who are afflicted with the craze for souvenirs, there is another sign, less poetic, more practical, reading, "It is dangerous to dig in the ruins." I keep a respectful distance from the crumbling wreckage of what was one of the architectural wonders of Northern Europe, the Cloth Hall of Ypres.

The Cloth Hall was the target for German guns for four terrible years, a symbol of British doggedness throughout those years, a symbol of British valor for all time to come. Here, Great Britain did one of her bravest bits in saving Belgium and the world. She need build no monument to her two hundred thousand dead, who fell in Flanders Fields! Their monument was built more than six hundred years ago, when Baldwin the Ninth Count of Flanders laid the cornerstone, in the exact year 1200, of what became the grandest and most graceful structure in the Low Countries. During the centuries it stood proudly, dominating the tranquil placid town that Ypres had become; stood in all its glory, when the Kaiser gave the signal for the wrecking of our beautiful old world.

The women here, as elsewhere, have been emancipated by the War; conducting trolley cars is new to them, but work as work has long been familiar to the Belgian women. The milkman has always been a woman, going from house to house with a big copper vessel full of fresh milk, pouring from it the quantity required by each customer. We were amazed to find so many fine old copper jars in Belgium; we visited shops crammed with wonderful specimens of the old ones. "Where did you get all this?" "We had it," they would always reply, "but we buried it while the Germans were in town."

A Beguinage is a secluded city within a city, inhabited by women known as Beguines. A Beguine is not a beggar; nor is a Beguinage a charitable institution. It is ▼ a place that offers home and quietude to women, who for any reason wish to dwell apart from worldly aims and interests.

They live in groups, like members of so many industrial clubs. They pay an alloted sum each year as dues; attend the services of the Catholic Church; do a fixed amount of work teaching poor children, visiting the sick, and sewing, and whatever they make is sold for their own account. The care of the kitchen falls upon all, in turn the table service is extremely

Bismarck lived here.

poetry. Its valley is a great storehouse of folk tales, myths, legends, and romance. It is a symbol of patriotism. It is the delight of childhood and the solace of old age. It was a classic river before the German states were born. It was Caesar's river long before it became a German defense. It has rolled its threatening current across the path of many would-be conquerors of the world. It has witnessed many savage victories and many pitiful defeats. It allowed Napoleon, wearing his buoyant boots of victory, to walk upon its waters. Later it became the symbol of Teutonic pride. And now it has become the symbol of the costliest victory humanity has ever won.

A tour of the Valley of the Rhine in 1919, the year following the Armistice, gave me double satisfaction. First, it enabled me to observe how this favorite region of old Germany looked in the period when it was dominated by her enemies, with streets and villages and bridges occupied by soldiers in the uniforms of France, Belgium, England, and the United States; and, second, it gave me an opportunity to observe what the War had done to the country, so alluring in its fascination in the days before the war.

My first impression was that the old attractions of the German's beloved Rhine were still there, unmarred by the devastating touch of war. The Rhineland cities, towns, and villages were all intact, undamaged, almost undisturbed by the great conflict. Vineyards and farms and fields were green, smiling, and productive. They seemed rich in the promise of a full and happy harvest. All this was very pleasant, but it offered a sad and dramatic contrast to what I had already seen, only a few days before, in undefeated Belgium and in victorious France. Victory had cost them dear, but defeat cost the Germans only loss of face—and hardly that, for they would not admit that they had

simplified. Each Beguine, like Old Mother Hubbard, has her own cupboard, which is far from bare. She brings her food from the kitchen, opens up her locker, draws out a little shelf and proceeds with her simple meal undisturbed and almost unobserved, for the open doors of the lockers screen the Beguines, one from another.

GERMANY

The Rhine has always been an object of affection to the German people. It is the source of much of their

A village on the Rhine.

been defeated. They did admit that the war was over, and claimed that they had asked for peace only in order to save the many lives that a continuation of the struggle would have cost.

1920 CONSTANTINOPLE

◀ This is one of the great bridges of the world, over it pass every day the most cosmopolitan and in some ways the most interesting multitudes to be observed anywhere in the wide world today. The Galata Bridge in Constantinople is a vast, moving ethnologic exhibition, well worth the small price of admission extracted by the toll collectors, who hold up each conveyance until placated by the payment of a filthy scrap of paper money, the value of which I never took the trouble to inquire.

JERUSALEM

Ever since Jerusalem was founded, it has been the prize fought for in war after war. It has fallen many times, its walls razed, its temples overturned, its people slain or exiled; but city after city has risen above the ruins of the older city overthrown.

No conqueror has been able to vanquish Zion's determination to exist. War has been powerless to wipe out Jerusalem. There is a vital hold on the eternal verities, in the City of David and in the people of Israel,

A leisurely dip in the Dead Sea. ▶

that nothing, either of time or circumstance, can suppress. War and Man have been compelled to recognize the indestructibility, the everlastingness of the Jews and Jerusalem, that old gray city on a hill, whose "light cannot be hid."

◄ Curly locks affected by the strictly Orthodox Jews of Jerusalem.

▼ In the heart of this crowded world of strangeness and color we find camels resting in sun-flooded hotel courtyards.

Jerusalem had a blizzard in February, 1920, the first ▼ one in two thousand years. It put the city to sleep. Snow itself is not entirely unknown, Jerusalem has experienced a few rare gentle flurries in the past. But a real snow storm, this was new, something astounding and alarming. A few structures collapsed under the unaccustomed weight of snow. Frightened folk shut themselves indoors as the life of the city came to an absolute standstill. But Jerusalem recovered from its chilly panic, and one of the many memorable and miraculous things that have happened in Jerusalem in modern times passed into history.

England is not Great Britain. England is not the British Empire, but England is and must remain the heart and soul of the world-wide federation of free peoples who speak her language, cherish her ideals, and give her loyal, respectful, self-respecting, and intelligent allegiance.

There is something thoroughbred about England, something that men of other nations are impelled to admire and respect even though they may resent and pretend to ridicule it. Nowhere in the world is there a land so rich in gentlemen.

This is where the big lights of the legal profession ▶ make their home. I enter a rather curious enclosure and pause in front of a window full of wigs. Several old wig-makers here—one grand old man has been making wigs for a generation, covering the brainiest brains of the profession.

◀ The shops along Bond Street are very elegant and very interesting. One shop window I passed had several coronets on display. I thought a coronet would be an interesting souvenir to bring back home and I went in to learn the prevailing price of coronets that day. But the salesman politely told me that the management bought these to oblige certain of their clients—but of course they would not *think* of selling them.

And the contrast between window and window! My word of honor—right next door was this display of ducks and drakes. And all along that fashionable thoroughfare you will find the cheesemongers, the butchers, etc. with their rather fragrant open-air shops.

◄ This charming little house is only four feet wide. I was told that the valet for whom it was built did not want the width of his dwelling to be any wider than his master's doorway.

STONEHENGE

Stonehenge is a colossal and enduring mystery. The wise men of successive centuries have striven to solve this mystery, but in vain. The name is said to be derived from a name given by the Saxons—Stanhengist—meaning "Hanging Stones."

No man knows for what purpose these great stones were erected on the low hill that looms above the wide and windswept Salisbury Plain. Some say that Stonehenge was the tomb of Constantine the Great, or a Roman temple, a Tuscan shrine, or a circle for Druidic serpent worship. But the latest theory advanced, and to me the most reasonable, is that Stonehenge was a temple for the worship of the sun. The arrangement and orientation of the mighty blocks suggest that the mysterious temple was a colossal prehistoric sun-dial and calendar stone, erected with careful regard to the direction of the sun's appearance on the morning of the summer solstice.

It is with a thrill of wonder that we look through one of the titanic trilithons—which opens like a portal of the fathomless past—and see, framed there against the blue of the heavens, a British military aviator cleaving the ancient skies with the most modern of all craft.

1922 THE YANGTZE RIVER IN CHINA

Our first impression of the Yangtze is of flat monotony. We might be on the lower reaches of the Mississippi. There is nothing to see and it isn't worth looking at. But we know that while the first thousand miles offer us little more than this—the next five hundred miles will reveal to us the glories of the Yangtze Gorges.

Imagine, if you will, moving slowly but irresistibly along and up an inclined floor of living, seething water against an eight-knot current, through a deep corridor cut in a range of mountains by a river that is furiously trying to reach the sea. Imagine yourself afloat on an aging steamer determined to take you and all things that venture out upon its swirling surface irrevocably downward with it, downward to the distant ocean, downward into the gaping whirlpools which have opened all about you, downward to destruction and oblivion in these awful depths. For what is drawn down into these sullen, gripping waters, never rises. The dead men of the Yangtze tell no tales because their bodies are never seen again.

1923 MOROCCO

Going up in the air is not a novelty for any of us now. We have all been up in the air—in so many different ways—since 1914, that we are now accustomed to Sky-Cruising—economically, financially, and otherwise.

But the Sky-Cruising I did this summer was for me a complete novelty, for in the aviation sense of the phrase I had never been "up in the air" before. I am not so sure that I am going soon again. I intend to rest upon—my wings, as it were.

But the thoughts one thinks, up there, do not make graceful verbal landings, down here—and the new descriptive eloquence with which I felt myself endowed—up there—as I soared from continent to continent, began missing on all cylinders the moment that our sky-larking car came down to earth.

We take off from Toulouse—not for reasons of alliteration but because Toulouse is the only town in France from which you can take off for Africa.

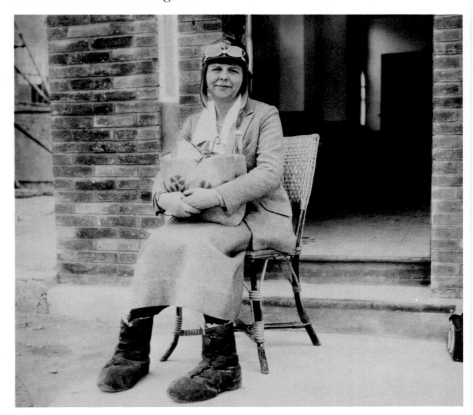

Margaret Holmes.

263

When you are starting for the first time to be an angel you naturally take along a lot of worry and anxiety. You do not always take your wife. I did—for reasons best known to the lady. I suspect she didn't care to trust me all alone up there among the other angels. Anyhow she had planned to go—and had been at some pains to provide a most inappropriate wardrobe for the trip. But she had amply provided against the possibility of getting cold feet.

And so away, over the fence and over the trees and toward the distant Pyrenees. The sensation is delightful. We scarcely know when we leave the ground—or when it leaves us. We are not conscious of climbing—and having climbed a few hundred feet we are no longer conscious of unusual speed, not until we pass a rushing train, leaving it behind so rapidly that it almost seems as if it must be going the other way. At this rate we shall be over the Pyrenees in a minute or two! But no! The plane banks suddenly to starboard and before

we know it we are going the other way—and worse, we seem to be descending the field from which we have just risen. The men at the hangars are rushing out—we grip the frail rim of the cockpit, the machine settles—touches earth, bumping over rough ground, slows down and taxis back to the very spot from which we started.

Resolved to be game, we ask the pilot if he has forgotten something. His reply sounds funny now, but we didn't find it funny then. He said, "There's a fly in the carburetor." And they proceed to look for the fly. They can't find that intrusive insect—so they trundle out another plane, transfer the mail sacks and our luggage and incidentally us—for passengers are the least important part of a mail plane's cargo—to that other air-bus, which is supposed to have its carburetor innocent of flies.

At least we hope so, for one unsuccessful get-away is all that a beginner's nerve is equal to. I am proud to say it never for a moment occurred to us to take the Ford bus back to town. If it had been a Rolls-Royce, perhaps—but to back out of our great adventure, in a Ford—we just could not admit the thought. And so, as in a dream one does the same thing over and over again—as if it were perfectly natural to keep on doing it, we repeat the performance of embarking and this time, with no fly in the carburetor, it's over the fence and over the trees and over the hills and toward the Pyrenees. We have climbed until we are so far from earth that we can judge neither our height, nor speed; riding the ether so naturally that flying seems to be the surest, safest, least exciting thing—on earth.

The pilot is too busy to tell us anything, and so we may but guess at what we see in the vast panorama that seems to unroll itself so slowly as we speed through the upper air, thousands of feet above the earth at ninety miles an hour.

◄ Within the Kasbah or fortress of the long ago, the French have re-created a veritable Moorish paradise—the likeness of the Moorish gardens of eight hundred years ago. Pictures may not convince you—but this Kasbah, in Rabat, surrounded by these battlemented walls, shaded by the grim Medersa Tower and refreshed by waters lifted from a well, this ancient place is one of the most delightful spots that I have ever lingered in.

———————

When I was in Morocco the first time the only wheeled vehicle in the entire empire was the state coach of the Sultan. Now many a low-born infant possesses a perambulator. ►

1924 ITALY

I've often been asked, "What is your favorite country?" My answer always is: "I have two favorite foreign countries—one in the Orient—Japan, and one in Europe—Italy." Why do I like them best? Above all because they are so good to look at. Because the history of each goes back to the dawn of their respective civilizations. Because the roots of their culture and their art are deep-set in the rich soil of the centuries. Because both are volcanic lands—and volcanic lands are always beautiful with the beauty that at times invites the jealous anger of the Gods.

Although no two lands could be more unlike than are Japan and Italy, no two peoples more dissimilar than are the Japanese and the Italians, both have for most of us an irresistible appeal.

The secret of the charm of both Japan and Italy lies in the fact that the beauty sought for and found by more artistic earlier generations has left its everlasting mark upon both lands which, despite the disturbing hand of progress, still offer to the eye pictures of enduring ancient dignity and loveliness unrivalled elsewhere in this changing modern world.

267

Some Roman graffiti, more elegant than most.

A Roman sculptor and his creation.

In a Roman park.

Arches in Naples.

Driving in the Italian Alps.

Mussolini with King Victor Emmanuel III.

"But is the Blue Grotto really blue?" everyone wants to know. My answer is this picture. The blueness is, of course, a luminous illusion. The rocks are not blue—and the water, if you pick it up, is colorless, but the sunshine of the Italian day, filtering through that crystal liquid, takes on this tone of beautiful unearthly azure for which the Blue Grotto or "La Grotta Azzura" of Capri is world-famous. [See colorplate on page 247]

Awaiting the appearance of Mussolini are delegations ▶ of Fascisti—combattenti—come from all the provinces of Italy to take part in a great "Adunata"—or gathering, in memory of their fallen comrades of the battle of Piave, the victory that turned the tide of the Great War. And, in addition, to pay tribute to their leader who now controls the destinies of the new Italy. Thirty thousand of them acclaim him as he appears on the high balcony of the Palazzo Venezia. From that balcony he speaks—so clearly and so forcibly, that we, here on a house-top on this far side of the wide piazza, can hear and understand all that he says. His voice is vibrant with an intensity that brings instant enthusiastic response to every word he utters. Never have I seen a speaker so sway so great an audience. What he says is brief and to the point—"There shall be liberty, but not liberty to mutilate our victory, not liberty to destroy the nation."

Mussolini was once a socialist, a communist, a radical, editor of the red paper called "Avanti," demanding the destruction of our social order. But he has seen the futility of all such doctrines, he knows now that it is only through bondage that men can come to freedom. We must be bound by law, by duty, by the necessity to labor, if we would be free to enjoy the blessings of order, peace, prosperity, and progress.

Ceylonese natives.

1925 CEYLON

That Ceylon was the site of the Garden of Eden is a popular belief. That Ceylon is still a paradise is an undisputed fact. Though lying near the southern tip of British India, Ceylon does not in any sense belong to India: it is a separate and unique country with its own picturesque civilization, its own ancient art and architecture, its own romantic legends and heroic history.

Imperial elephants in the Palace compound of the King of Siam.

ANGKOR WAT

◄ The amazing Angkor Wat, the crowning creation of the Golden Age of the Khmers. This apotheosis of a forgotten art dates from the end of the thirteenth century.

It was not quite completed when the mighty Empire mysteriously fell, the population ebbed away, the jungle crept in and reclaimed the site, and the glories of Angkor began their slumber of six centuries here in this silent tropic wilderness.

There is a troupe of ballet dancers at Angkor Wat, poor village girls, well-trained in the one great surviving art of Old Cambodia, the Lakhon or the Classic Dance. Their teachers are two old women, who were once royal dancers in the harem of the King. These village girls evoke for me the remote ceremonies of the vanished past. Thus did they make the life of Angkor animate to modern eyes. Thus did they greet and offer tribute to the ancient, half-forgotten gods, for in their dance I saw repeatedly that classic gesture of a gracefully uplifted but uncanny hand, the finger and thumb poised according to the canons of a classic art, an offering of lotus blossoms in a gesture of pride, humil-
◄ ity, and adoration to the gods of a great people.

1926 HOLLAND

Here at Scheveningen the wives of local fishermen ►
appear on Sunday, on this fashionable promenade, dressed and coifed just as their mothers were a hundred years ago. No short skirts for the fisher maidens—no cloche hats to spoil the quaint and pretty coifs that so well set off their calm and honest faces. They live in Scheveningen and yet they seem to be in no way touched by this modernizing flood of changing fashions which has even brought the Charleston to these classic sands.

Scheveningen, watering-place of The Hague.

Aerial view of the polders.

We always think of Holland as a place of wooden shoes and windmills. Well, the wooden shoes, the klompen, will undoubtedly be worn for many years to come—but the windmills of Holland, alas for art and artists, are doomed to disappear. There are still many of them standing but very few in use. Those which, like this one in Rotterdam, are used as sawmills will persist. But the vast majority, used merely for pumping water from the low polders up to the high canals, are being rapidly supplanted by the far more effective gasoline pumps of today.

I ought to give you now a peroration inspired by the achievements of these people of the Netherlands in civilization, in war, in letters and in art—praising the courage of their heroes, the wisdom of their statesmen, the genius of their painters, and the industry and patience of the humbler subjects of Queen Wilhelmina, and paint rosy pictures of their future—but I am more inclined simply to let these two small Dutch folk of the rising generation assure you by the brave look in their honest eyes—that all is well with Holland and the Dutch.

A youthful artist poses for the camera.

Never shall I forget the trouble and excitement occasioned by my attempt, some years ago, to get a real hot bath in the lodgings I had taken—before discovering that there was no modern plumbing on the premises. "Un bain, Monsieur? Mais parfaitement! I will make the bath to come at five o'clock this afternoon," said the obliging concierge when I expressed a desire for total immersion. "But I want the bath now, this morning, before breakfast," I insisted. "Impossible, Monsieur, it requires time to prepare and to bring, but it will be superb—your bath—the last gentleman who took one a month ago enjoyed his very much. You will see, Monsieur, that when one orders a bath in Paris, one gets a beautiful bath—it will be here at four o'clock."

At four, a man, or rather a pair of legs, came staggering up my stairs—five flights, by the way—with a full-sized zinc bath tub, inverted and concealing the head and shoulders and half the body of the miserable owner of those legs. The tub was planted in the middle of my room; a white linen lining was adjusted; sundry towels and a big bathing sheet, to wrap myself in after the ordeal, were ostentatiously produced. Then came the all-important operation of filling the tub. Two pails, three servants, and countless trips down to the hydrant, several floors below, at last did the trick: the tub was full of cold water. "But I ordered a hot bath." "Patience, Monsieur, behold here is the hot water!" Whereupon the bath man opens a tall zinc cylinder that looks like a fire extinguisher and pours about two gallons of hot water into that white-lined tub—result a tepid bath—expense sixty cents—time expended two hours, for the tub had to be emptied by dipping out the water and carrying it away, pail after pail. Then the

proud owner of the outfit slung his pails on his arms, put his tub on his head like a hat, and began the perilous descent of my five flights of stairs. I had had enough of primitive Paris—I moved to costlier quarters where tubbing was not wonderingly regarded as an Anglo-Saxon extravagance, to be indulged in more as a matter of monthly ostentation than as a joyful daily duty.

Paris has many modern conveniences.

A bar in Montmartre.

synonym for the night-prowling criminal of Paris—the man who stabs and kills for the pleasure of the thing—the man who lets a woman work for him—pays her with blows, and when in need of some excitement, waits in a dark street to strike and rob a passer-by, more for the pleasure of killing than for the profit of the robbing. One night a gallant friend of mine, returning hotelward from a long night of sight-seeing, was stopped in a dark street by three Apaches. He was alone—they were in force, and therefore bold. They swaggered up in front of him, instead of sneaking on him from behind. One said, "Tiens, my friend, nous sommes des Apaches—we are Apaches!" Striving to strike terror to his heart at mention of the fearsome name. "Bien, my friends," said mon ami, "c'est bien, moi, je suis Nick Cartaire—I am Nick Carter!" whereupon the dumbfounded French "Indians" fled in dismay.

The Apache of Paris is no Indian: he has assumed the name and acquired the bloodthirsty instincts, but he lacks the nobler attributes of the red man of the plains. How did the "bad man," the tough, the thug of Paris get his trans-Atlantic title? He took it, so they say, from the American dime novel. The famous thrillers, the "Nick Carter Tales" of blood and thunder which have been the inspiration of the American messenger boy, were translated into French and republished in Paris. The gaudy pictures on the covers of those books appealed to the adventurous Bowery class of Paris. The stories suited the "bad man" of the outer boulevards, the Apache on the war-path or in quest of blood became their most honored type of lawlessness, and Nick Carter a much feared and highly respected personification of law and order. So Apache in time became a

The famous Artists and Models Ball—Le Bal des ▶ Quat'z Arts, is held every year in Paris, and is—well, it's just not what we are accustomed to here at home. I can't quite see our people going in for a real Quat'z Arts Ball. I went to one. I saw things I never dreamed that I should ever live to see!

I remember that my ticket to the Ball cost me twenty-seven dollars and was worth it. Ordinarily, one goes to a ball to see fine clothes—to see what people are wearing—to study the latest styles—but one goes to the Ball of the Four Arts in Paris to see fine figures—to see what people are *not* wearing—to study, not the latest, but the earliest and most primitive mode of dress. It takes you back to the pre-fig leaf period, to the days in the garden of Eden, before the fall of man, when all was innocence, and modesty was still a word uncoined.

The famous "running of the bulls" in Pamplona.

It was in Seville that I saw my first bull fight. "Never again," said I to myself. But I remained to watch the bloody scenes in the arena—and to learn to overlook the cruel and gory aspects of the national sport and for the moment, find peculiar pleasure in the amazing skill and daring of the toreros, banderilleros, and matadores.

"Death in the Afternoon" can be counted upon to hold your attention no matter how little you like Hemingway. I hold no brief for the bull fight—it is a horrid, beastly, cruel, and barbarous performance— but if you go to three corridas in succession, I defy you not to want to go again. Bull fights are like olives, you don't like your first one, but in spite of every decent sentiment which animates you, at your fourth corrida it's ten to one you will be thrilled. There is something alluring about even a thrill of horror—and thrills give pleasure even though you are ashamed of them.

There was in those days another national sport in Spain—a nocturnal sport. But my first contact with it came by day. In a first-class railway compartment I occupied one of the eight seats. I felt a feverish sensation; I was hot under the collar. Presently my *vis-à-vis*, a Spanish gentleman, leaned forward, plucked something from my neck and tossed it out the window saying, "Permit me to quit you of an evil thing." I was grateful but embarrassed. The other passengers, amused, shrank away from me as far as space permitted. I tried to explain that I had come direct from the best and cleanest hotel in the last town. This did not seem to reassure them. However, it was with pleasure that presently I leaned forward and said to one of

A religious procession in Pamplona.

283

A horse is gored.

The banderillero.

them, "Permit me in turn to quit *you* of an evil thing." By this time we were all feverish. Standing up, we examined the seats on which we had been sitting. The cushions were alive with "evil things." We staged a massacre and flung the corpses from the windows. Then when the fray was over, desirous of warning future travelers, we unscrewed from the walls the little frames that held notices to passengers like, "Dangerous to lean out," and "Smoking prohibited." These we reversed and replaced after printing clearly on the back of each, *"Atención—Hay millones de chinches en este compartimento"*—"Attention! There are millions of bed bugs in this compartment."

But for me, the worst was still to come. In Vallodolid I lodged in the best hotel—God save the mark! At midnight I rang for the maid and requested a change of room. Leaving my luggage where it was, my feverish carcass was put to bed elsewhere. At one A.M. I again demanded another room. At two A.M. I rang again. The maid, her patience exhausted, inquired why I wished to move from room to room. When I explained, she seemed astonished. "But Señor, you ought to know, they are in *all* our rooms. *This* is the season!" There was a train at three A.M. I took it, after retrieving my belongings left in the first infested room that I had occupied, where in my bed lay a caballero, or at any rate, a native guest, a late arrival, snoring serenely, unbothered by the chinches. He knew it was the season. Things are better now and there are clean hotels in Spain for fussy travelers.

THE moment.

The Strand.

Tower Bridge traffic.

1929 LONDON

◄ The wonder is that London parks are not packed with people all the time—that there is room for all the quietude and calm. It is strange indeed when we think of the pressure of the dense multitude without that this great vacuum, this area of land unoccupied and empty, should not be filled instantly to overflowing by an irresistible inrush of humanity from the congested regions round about.

This happens only now and then, as a result of some slight socialistic agitation of that encircling human sea. Wave after wave of decently dressed and earnest people roll quietly in from the surrounding streets, settle into a calm sea of faces upturned toward the orator, who is thundering a condemnation of the existing order of things. I listened in amazement to the most outspoken abuse of the government, yet not a protest came from any of the many bobbies within earshot. The working-folk listen attentively, applaud with discrimination, and when the show is over march off as they came, in orderly, well-ordered ranks, obeying every behest of the polite but firm policemen.

287

◄ From this point in Trafalgar Square we look up at the statue of Admiral Lord Nelson standing seventeen feet high atop this column. Some critics say this is one of the worst pieces of sculpture, but then it is so high that one never sees Lord Nelson anyway except from the top of a neighboring column which no one ever climbs.

1930   T U N I S

Tunis, which is so rich in color and sights, surprises us ▶ with delightful bits of oriental architecture such as this.

One part of Tunis is completely Europeanized. We ▼ might be in a lesser city of continental France if it were not for the peculiar costumes of the passersby. The Jewesses of Tunis wear not only the veil, but these peg-top trousers as well. So many women affect this dress that they attract only the attention of the tourist.

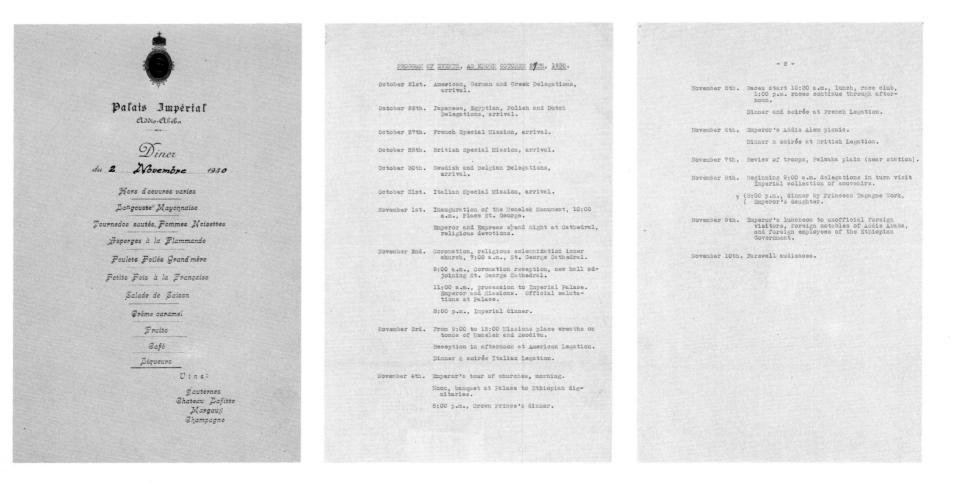

ETHIOPIA (The Coronation of Haile Selassie)

To reach Ethiopia, I had to go from Djibouti to Addis Ababa as a stowaway on the special train belonging to H.R.H. the Duke of Gloucester, and his brilliant suite of generals and admirals.

I was the only photographer allowed to take pictures in the Imperial enclosure. This I accomplished by a gentle ruse: suitably attired in high hat, tails, a pair of impeccable spats, and an aristocratic air—I ventured forth. Since I looked the part of a gentleman, no one challenged my right to be there diffidently juggling my tripod in the stifling 104-degree heat.

Perhaps the list of events for the Coronation may be of interest, and the original menu, too. Even two slave girls seem to enjoy the commotion and spectacle. [See colorplate on page 245]

Queen Mary and King Doug at home at Pickfair.

1931 HOLLYWOOD

The metropolis of Moviedom. A little like a journey to the land of the Arabian Nights. Our magic carpet drops us into the central square of old Bagdad before the Palace of the King. I happened later, jestingly, to tell an Englishman that I had stopped over to Hollywood to take luncheon with the King and Queen. "Oh, not really?" he protested. "Yes, really," I insisted, "with Queen Mary and King Doug." We lunched that day at the royal table in King Doug's Chinese banquet hall, where every day a dozen of the great, near great or would-be great are to be found enjoying the bounty of Robin Hood and Little Annie Rooney.

On the lot, across the way from the Palace of Bagdad, ▼ the New York slums rise in all their musty ugliness. Here the motion picture "Street Scene" is being shot.

Hollywood is filled with fantasy, from a fabulous pre-miere like that of "Hell's Angels" at Grauman's Chinese, to one of the miniature golf courses that have become such a craze, to anything-but-ordinary-looking sandwich shops and drive-ins with their com-plements of "car-hop" waitresses whose good looks proclaim them to be hopeful would-be "movie stars."

1932 J A V A

They say that there is nothing new under the sun. This may be true, but the traveler always finds cause to doubt it—especially if his wanderings lie under the tropic sun.

The costume of the Javanese girl is exquisitely simple and supremely comfortable—no hooks and eyes—no whalebone—no high strangling collar—just the quaintly colored sarong of complex design folded around her form. No shoes upon her feet, but in her ears a pair of barbarous earrings, brutally bulky, thrust through the lobes which are pierced to receive the peg-like stems, a full half-inch in diameter. Thus dame fashion grips the maid of Java only by the ear.

"Streets of Paris," the nudist colony attraction.

The Flit guns brigade.

The Hollywood concession.

1933 THE CENTURY OF PROGRESS EXPOSITION IN CHICAGO

Chicago has offered a splendid spectacle, in commemoration of her eventful Century of Progress—of the hundred years that have elapsed since a little company of pioneers housed in shacks and cabins round about a frontier fort resolved to incorporate their community. There and then, in 1833, was born the town and four years later, the City of Chicago. It has lived—dangerously and magnificently. It has grown up, but not grown old. The spirit of youth still animates it. It has suffered much—it has done great things—it is still firm in its resolve to do still greater things—and in testimony of its faith in itself, in America, and in the happy future of the world in which we live and in the civilization that we have developed, it will, on the first day of June of this good year, 1933, open the gates of a Great Exposition to which it bids the whole world welcome.

297

"It won't be long now before we see the golden domes of Moscow," I say to my friend as we pass what looks like a suburban station. But the golden domes do not appear. Instead, the tops of smoking chimneys and the ugly, endless walls of factories and flats. We might be coming into Manchester or Pittsburgh. What has become of the colorful oriental capital of ancient Muscovy? What has become of lots of things that used to be in Russia? My impressions of thirty-three years ago have already begun to revise themselves.

The train pulls into a big busy station. Before my belongings have been touched by any porter, a tall, spare, tired-looking man inquires in English, "Are you traveling Intourist?" He takes charge of me and my baggage, and I follow him to the exit, where he stows me and my belongings into a brand new Lincoln touring car. At my request, my German companion, who is to spend his hours between trains with me, is also taken under the Intourist wing. Away, along wide crowded streets, we whirl. Much motor traffic, many horse-drawn carts, and on all the sidewalks, what seems like a procession. From curbs to shop fronts, every sidewalk is crowded.

"Why all these crowds?" I ask. "Is this a holiday—is there to be a special demonstration or procession?"

"No, these are just people on their way to work."

Throughout my stay I never lost this impression of highly animated streets and overcrowded sidewalks. As for the long trains of trolley cars, with four heads leaning out of each window, with interiors piled full of humanity, and with swaying bunches of men and boys and women clinging to every platform-end and hitch-hikers holding on astern, the electric surface system of Moscow makes the New York subway in the rush hour look like a deserted village. There is no special rush hour in Moscow; it is like that all day and far into the night. I had heard that the Soviets were building a subway in Moscow. I thought this was mere bravado, something to tell the world about. I can tell the world right now that if any city ever needed a subway, this overcrowded, ever-growing city centering on the Kremlin is the one that stands most urgently in need of underground urban transportation.

There are practically no taxicabs. You either ride as an Intourist protégé in a lordly, balloon-tired Lincoln over the roughly cobbled streets, or else you become —after long waits for a chance to shove yourself aboard or to grab a handhold on a trolley car—one of those human sardines inside or one of those dangling scraps of humanity that cling precariously to the outside of those antiquated rattle-boxes.

There are no privately owned motor cars. You must belong to some Soviet organization to be privileged to use or to have the use of an official car. Of course, "a gentleman can always walk"—but there are no gentlemen in Russia. Or if there be, they do not dare acknowledge the fact or look the part. The epithet "gentleman" is not one that any Soviet citizen of Moscow cares to have pinned on him—it smacks too much of the old régime. No one can afford to be suspected of being a "bourgeois gentilhomme."

All Moscow looks like one vast red flag on the last day of April. The May Day decorations are completed and in place. They are astonishing.

Along the front of the unfinished fourteen-story hotel has been erected the most unbelievable decoration of all. The effect is that of a red flag, ten stories high and perhaps two hundred feet long, almost completely masking the wide façade of the high structure. Upon the flag appear gigantic portrait heads: that of Lenin is fully nine stories high; that of Stalin, a little less enormous; those of the fourteen other leaders of the Communist Party range from one to three stories in height. As a political portrait gallery, this surpasses in sheer magnitude anything of the kind I have ever seen.

For all the nations of the world save one, the First of May has for a long time been a date with sinister implications. Governments have dreaded the First of May, kings, presidents and parliaments have breathed easier on the morning of the second day of this beautiful spring month.

In Russia, since 1917, the First of May has been the Red Letter Day of the year—the national, and even international great holiday of the new deal as it is understood under the red flag. Just imagine being privileged to wave a red flag in public and cheer for Communism—and get away with it! It can't be done in Union Square, in Hyde Park, or the Place de la Bastille. But in the Red Square of Moscow everything goes on the First of May and goes with a most astonishing effect.

I have witnessed many thrilling demonstrations. Never have I seen anything to equal the impressive, menacingly beautiful spectacle presented in the Red Square from early morning until late evening on May first, 1934. More than one million seven hundred thousand Russian men, women, and children took part in it. The few thousands of spectators of the show were hopelessly outnumbered. It seemed unfair to

give so big a show before so limited an audience. But I was glad to be there in that audience.

From Odessa we motored out into the country to visit a collective farm. The road was bad, the heat and dust almost unbearable—and when we reached the central village of this communized farm, we saw little to convince us that Russian agriculture is on its way to anything more than hard work and mediocre crops. The buildings, granaries, stables, and "garage" for the tractor that had not yet arrived were tumble-down, the horses skinny, and the farm implements crude and in poor condition. The villagers looked well-fed and seemed to be doing very little. There was a rude clubroom adorned with pictures of Lenin and Stalin and an out-of-door theater with a covered stage and wooden benches lined up in the garden. The whole effect was pitiful. If this is the sort of thing the Soviets arrange as a showplace to impress the foreign visitor, they have wasted time and effort.

The most interesting thing I saw was the baby check-room where some forty or fifty infants were left every day while the mothers are working in the fields. The babes were all asleep in neat little cots. Three capable-looking women were in charge of this collective crèche, and if as a mere man I may venture an observation, let me say that the babies seemed far better off than if they had been left at home in charge of aged and incompetent peasant grandmothers—or of the older children of the family. With her precious younglings checked in for the day at this quiet, well-administered cottage home, the mother of a family is free to go and give her best effort to her day's work in the fields, unworried by what may be happening at home. This sort of thing must improve the morale of the women workers and I cannot see in it any attempt to break up the family home. Sick, crying, ill-cared-for

301

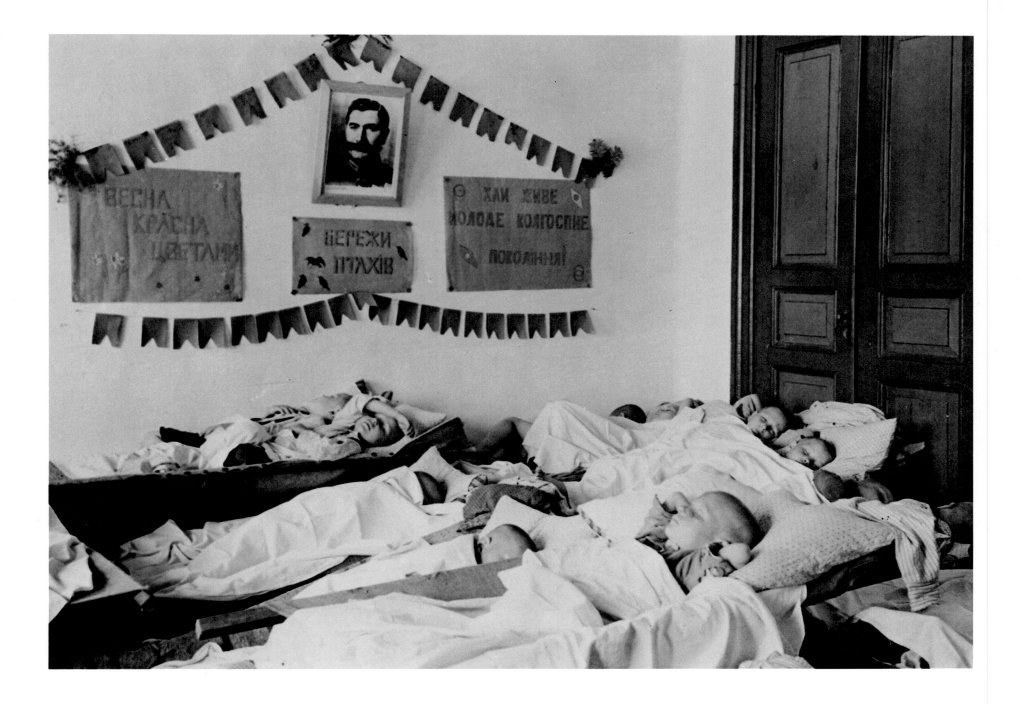

kiddies in a home of poverty seem to me more of a menace to the peace and permanence of that home than contented, well-cared-for babies spending their days in charge of nurses who have no other duties and are trained for this, their special task.

In the city of Kharkov, in the square before the Red Army Club—a sort of colossal many-storied Y.M.C.A.—I note a number of kiosks surrounded by eager crowds. "This is the book mart," says the local guide. "Thousands of books are sold here every week. Our people, now that they can read, are all eager to learn all that they can about everything."

We drive out into the surrounding countryside outside Moscow to visit the estate of Count Sheremetyev, called Ostankino. The palace was built by serfs, the furniture and decorations designed, made, and installed by serfs. The former mistress of Ostankino, and of the Count, was a lovely serf, an actress whose name is as picturesque as it is trying to the foreign tongue. Her name was Parasha Zhemchugova. Everything about the palace looks gay and cheaply second rate, but we were assured that Parasha was a first-rate player and that the troupe of serf players who acted with her for the entertainment of the Count's distinguished and Imperial guests were worthy of the lovely star whom they supported. The palace, with its private theater and its lovely gardens, is now the resort of proletarian excursionists from the neighboring capital.

I have figured it out that if I had ordered and consumed in New York as much caviar as came my way in my three weeks in Russia, it would have cost me, at New York per-portion-prices, about eighty-four dollars—more than one-third of the total cost of my twenty-one day tour in Russia. Of course, if you don't like caviar, you can't very well make this comforting mental deduction which reduces your daily expense—for all the *necessities* of Russian travel and sojourn—to a point where you begin to feel that you have the best of a big bargain. Thus, during my first hours in Moscow, I do not have to fall back upon the nuts and chocolate and other nutritious and portable things with which a thoughtful and forewarned wife had loaded one of my several suitcases.

Before supper, I had enjoyed another kind of feast—a feast of beauty. Two tickets for the evening performance of the Bolshoi Theater had been assigned me—one for the blonde young woman who had been my guide and interpreter throughout the morning. For these seats I was charged about four dollars and a half apiece. They were good seats—

305

where I like them for a ballet, right down in the front row. I am not *very* bald. The front row has been my favorite row ever since my early hirsute youth. I was glad to have the extra seat for my girl-guide. I felt that I needed some one to answer questions during my first evening in a Russian theater. My earlier visits to Moscow had been in midsummer when the opera and all the regular theaters were closed and the only entertainment was in the form of vaudeville and concerts in the open-air or summer garden theaters. Thus I had never seen a Russian ballet on a Russian stage. I had been thrilled by Pavlova and Mordkin in America—and by the Diaghilev dancers in Paris—and I was eager to see one of the stages on which those dancers had won their fame at home.

The Bolshoi Theater is a superb structure with a noble classic portico. The auditorium is one of the most grandiosely pleasing in the world. It looks a little bit run down at present but the effect of the ensemble is superb. Six shallow balconies curve one above another in graceful horse-shoes from orchestra to roof. They seem to hold only boxes and every seat in every box is filled. Apparently there are extra seats in many boxes. In some, people are standing. Every seat in the house is occupied. There are no ushers. You "locate" your place with the aid of large floor-plans in the lobbies. Then you make your way to it as best you can. To my astonishment, there are very few mix-ups. Very few spectators put themselves into the wrong seats and when they do, they always admit their mistake and move smilingly to the place where they belong. There are no arguments and no need to call an attendant to referee disputes.

In the vast, deep orchestra pit are about a hundred musicians. They are not well dressed. Nobody in the place is well dressed. Everybody looks seedy or shoddy, many ill-kempt, and not a few look dirty. I was not putting on any "dog" myself. My black sack suit was four years old and shiny at the elbows. My shoes were three years old—a well-loved pair of comfortable old friends which I had not dared to polish. But alas! My shirt was white—and clean—and my white wing collar stood out like a challenge to the whole U.S.S.R. I was painfully conscious of the unconscionable cleanness of that shirt and of the dazzling whiteness of that collar. I felt as Berry Wall might feel if he should chance to find himself marooned at the *Marché aux Puces* in Paris. I wanted to rush out and roll over in the dirt and come back to my seat socially improved.

But to my astonishment, no one seemed to pay any attention to me. There were no resentful glances in the direction of this clean-looking *"sale bourgeois."* There were no nudgings. Nobody seemed to be saying, "Get onto the guy with the high collar." Nor did my fair companion seem to find either pride or distress in my appearance. In fact, she looked pretty fine herself. She was easily the best looking and the best dressed woman in the audience, although her dress was a simple and inexpensive street frock. Near us sat a rather frowsy looking couple, working folk fresh from their labors at some factory, though "fresh" is not the word.

"How," I asked, "can people like that afford to pay for seats like ours, which you tell me cost about four dollars and a half?"

"Oh, they doubtless get their seats for nothing as a kind of bonus or reward for work well done—or if they buy them, they pay in rubles and if they are the right kind of workers, their rubles are worth more than the rubles of workers who have not proved themselves good workers. You see, certain favored categories of workers are permitted to buy seats at special low prices. The cost of your seat depends on who *you* are, not where *it* is."

"How much money is there in the house?" I inquire as I survey the auditorium, by this time packed from pit to dome.

"No one can tell—it all depends—but the performances are not given for profit. They are given for the cultural benefit to be derived by those who attend. The artists are well paid by the State—better paid than almost any other class of workers. They are workers too, and proud to do their artistic work for audiences made up of those who perform, not the harder—for no work is harder, more difficult than that of the artist—but the rougher work of our heavy industries."

I try to conjure up the brilliant audiences of the Imperial days which once filled this same auditorium. No trace of gold lace now, no gleam of pearls, glitter of diamonds, rustle of silks, no intoxicating perfumes. Just folks—tired, a little soiled, a little smelly, but all eager, expectant, and strange as it seems, intelligent of eye—as they wait for the rising of the curtain.

Up it goes, revealing a rich, mellow vision of the Paris of long ago. The performance is not to be an opera. It is to be a melodrama in pantomime entitled, "Esmeralda." It is Victor Hugo's "Hunchback of Notre Dame," done as a ballet. The idea seems absurd. The performance is superb. Never have I seen a stage more marvelously alive with beauty, color, movement, drama, and surprise. I have been a theater-goer all my life. Never have I seen anything like this Esmeralda ballet at the Bolshoi Theater. It took my breath away. They piled effect upon effect, surprise upon surprise—there was always something unexpected doing in an unexpected way. The mere dynamics of the thing stunned me. Seemingly power enough to run all the factories of Moscow was expended by those hundreds of dancers on the enormous stage—power so beautifully controlled, so exquisitely co-ordinated that it created poetry and drama there before our eyes. I had expected much of the Russian ballet on its own famous stage. I was not disappointed. The setting, costumes, properties all had a look of richness which harmonized with the mellow, gilded splendor of the auditorium but contrasted vividly with the aspect of the earnest, ill-clad folk that packed the theater and looked and listened, as their eyes and ears were filled with a revelation of beauty not of their world, a beauty bequeathed them by the Imperialistic past.

And yet today, this glorious thing of wonder and of beauty that is the Russian ballet, is their very own—for the proletariat of Russia is now dictator of the ballet as of all other things within the borders of the Soviet Union. And the proletariat supports and enjoys this glory and splendor of their theater, and seemingly appreciates even the finer shades of meaning which the artists are striving so magnificently to express. In the old days that audience and that performance would have been miles apart. Today, that performance brings that audience of toilers within thrilling distance of the dramatically sublime.

Joan of Arc was held prisoner in this tower in Rouen.

A ruined castle stands in its moat in the town of Fougères.

Many French artists have painted in the quaint fishing village of Honfleur.

1935 NORMANDY AND BRITTANY

In the changing Old World, one corner remains delightfully unchanged. The ancient provinces of northwestern France retain today the characteristics and charm of a world that used to be. For any traveler weary of the gay routine of Paris and the gorgeous frivolities of the Riviera, a journey into the France of Yesterday will come as a novel experience.

The homes of the world-conquering Normans and of the sea-conquering Bretons must be visited, for quiet charm still dwells there and the Past is still alive.

◄ This medieval structure, the Abbey of Mont Saint-Michel, rises from its rocky islet in the waters of the Bay of Brittany. Gazing seaward from the Norman coast, we behold a mighty rock, crowned with monasteries,

Mont Saint-Michel.

churches, palaces, and towers, outlined against the evening sky. The upper extremity of this bay is but a sort of estuary—a vast plain of sand which every day is twice covered by the sea and twice by it abandoned. The tides are phenomenal. On this bay at Granville a difference between high and low water of over fifty feet is frequently recorded. The tides of March and September have wiped out of existence many a seaside farm. It is said that at times the sea rushes in across the sands with such rapidity that the fleetest of horses could not outstrip the waves in the race for life and safety.

It has been proved that before this region became a part of the bay it was a forest, extending far beyond Mont Saint-Michel to other islands, then only hills, which now lie far out from the shore. For centuries the northwest coast of France has been undergoing a gradual subsidence. Recently there was discovered at a depth of ten feet or so beneath these sands a portion of a paved roadway, as well as a human skull and three skulls of a species of wild oxen, the aurochs, an animal which as early as the time of Caesar had ceased to exist in occidental Gaul. Entire trees perfectly preserved have frequently been found. These facts prove the existence of the antique forest and the profound transformations which this region has passed through. Only Mont Saint-Michel and a few minor islands have survived, thanks to their rocky bases.

A harbor scene in Audierne. The boats are in readiness to go out after bluefish.

1936 SOUTH AMERICA

South America was once much farther away than Europe. Now it has become almost our next-door neighbor, nearer to us in time than any part of the Old World. We may dine in New York one evening and in South America the next and go on dining in a different country every evening of our trip.

▲ A street scene in Mexico City combines the familiar and the exotic.

A street scene in Santiago, Chile, features another old ▲ friend from the movies.

The power of Hollywood is felt around the world. This ▶ spot for refreshment is in Buenos Aires, Argentina.

1937 SOUTH AFRICA

For many years, "Who's Who" had said, "Burton Holmes, traveler and lecturer, has traveled everywhere but South Africa." So, I decided to find a country audiences would like to hear about, and, at the same time, wipe out the line about never visiting South Africa. I sailed in May, and as soon as I reached Cape Town, I cabled "Who's Who":

"Lafayette, I am here."

Most people have the wrong impression of Africa. All of the continent is not jungle land with lions chewing up zebras. Cape Town, Johannesburg, and Durban are large, thriving cities with splendid streets, buildings, fine hotels, and residences.

This elaborately dressed Zulu and his wheeled conveyance, the "Zulu Taxi," combine to create a strange ritual fabricated entirely for tourist eyes. ▲

◄ We have been given images of the natives as drumbeating savages and naive innocents of nature, stereotypes quickly being broken by the influx of travelers to these countries. Exotic scenes can still be found, however, by those who seek them out.

1938 GERMANY

Just as in Japan and Italy, ambitious German leaders are using the schools to debauch the rising generation, to instill the poison of the "Master Race" complex, and to awaken and strengthen in the young those dormant, brutal instincts that are, alas, innate. Loyalty to Fuehrer, Duce, or "Son of Heaven" become the religion of the moment. To die for The Leader is the highest duty. Millions of deluded men have been privileged to fulfill that duty.

Although Burton Holmes traveled and lectured for almost twenty more years, the world he knew and loved was largely changed by World War II. Thus we end our volume at this point with his own triumphant affirmation of a life well spent.

GENOA CALDWELL

EPILOGUE: ON TRAVELING

"To travel is to possess the world." These words I have set down in many an autograph collector's book.

They are, I think, true words. I know that through travel I have possessed the world more completely, more satisfyingly than if I had acquired the whole earth by purchase or by conquest.

There is no implication of selfishness in the kind of possession of which I speak. Whoever possesses the world through travel takes naught from any man. No one is the poorer because you have made the whole world yours.

You have gained everything, but you are no monopolist. The wealth is there for all to share. It is not yours alone. Without claiming ownership of anything, you may issue reports about your annual income of delights and satisfactions. You may let others into the secret of your realized ambitions. You may invite all men and women to travel with you in imagination and they too may feel that they, like you, are rich in vivid mental pictures of places worth going to, of people worth knowing, of things that are world-famous.

One great advantage of possessing the world through travel is that one may enjoy all the satisfactions of possession without the responsibilities of ownership. Now, in days when our most valuable assets become or threaten to become our most crushing liabilities, it is good to contemplate property which cannot depreciate but must increase in value, property which cannot be taxed by federal government, or state or city authorities, property which calls for no repairs or alterations.

The only things I own which are still worth what they have cost me are my travel memories, the mind-pictures of places which I have been hoarding like a happy miser for more than half a century. There are no storage charges on this kind of property. No one can steal it from you. No conflagration can consume it. No catastrophe can destroy or even damage it. It is a part of you and you are absolute master of it and free to draw upon it every day and every hour for generous dividends of satisfaction.

In the past I have reproached myself for my extravagance, for lack of foresight, for disregard of proper provision for the future. My wise friends saved and economized, went without things they wanted, denied themselves the costlier pleasures of the table, the bouquet of vintage wines and the, to me, supreme joy of going places, seeing things, and taking possession through travel of the whole wide world.

And now where are we? We, they and I, are all at the same dead-end of life's highway. They are weighted down by all the leaden burdens of their golden hopes gone wrong. They have their memories but these are memories of wise, dull, and frugal days of systematic piling up of hard-earned dollars in safe places where those dollars would increase and multiply and be there to console for all the pleasures that their owners had denied themselves and all the fun that they had missed.

I, too, have nothing but my memories, but I would not exchange my memories for theirs. I have possession of a secret treasure upon which I can draw at will. I can bring forth on the darkest day, bright diamonds of remembered joys, diamonds whose many facets reflect some happy dream that has come true, a small ambition gratified, a long-sought sensation, caught and savored to the full, a little journey made, an expedition carried to success, a circumnavigation of the globe accomplished.

Yes, it is good to have possessed the world through travel. And it is good to rest, with nearly all of one's dreams realized. Dreams of going, seeing, and doing most of the things that seemed worth-while—good to know that you have in your own way possessed the world.

Burton Holmes died in July of 1958, and was cremated at his own request. His ashes were deposited in his favorite Siamese urn.